Opera Houses
of the World

Opera Houses
of the World

Thierry Beauvert

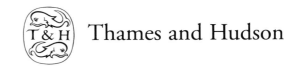Thames and Hudson

Contents

Study by Giuseppe Borsato for the decoration of the imperial box of the Fenice (1837).

Foreword

In the beginning was Vitruvius, who first established, at the outset of our era, the canons of classical theatre, which became almost axiomatic. They prevailed from Epidaurus to Vicenza or Sabbionetta, from Pompeii to Bayreuth, leaving architects to draw their lessons from history. In the 20th century, this respect for the ancients would even go so far as to rummage through history's attic and recover a few acoustical relics already abandoned in their own time, among them resonating jars placed under every seat and a stream of water running down the center of the orchestra stalls. Rome fell, but the theatre was reborn in the 17th century as opera. The genre came into the world with a silver spoon in its mouth, thanks to the Gonzagas in Mantua, the Medicis in Florence, and the Farneses in Parma, who hovered over its cradle and made it a court art. Later on, as a result, opera would often find it expedient to accept the will of a prince, who, in turn, might offer to enthrone it at the heart of the city, and sometimes even to endow it with the coveted title of palace—unless at the whim of a queen it found a niche under the foliage of a royal park at Versailles or Drottningholm. Beginning with the last days of the Enlightenment, the power of a nation could almost be measured by the strength of its opera companies. From Milan to Dresden, from Paris to Vienna, the great cities of Europe gave birth to grand opera houses which became the envy of the world, spawning imitations far and wide, some veritable clones, such as the mock Palais Garniers in Hanoi and Santiago. Yet theatre needed to consider its future, and so, in the wake of Richard Wagner, many architects began to experiment, as in the rapturous sail-like silhouette of the Sydney Opera House, or in the radical renovation of the old theatres in Lyons and Brussels, or yet the great leap

Staircase hall of the Opera House of Rio de Janiero.

forward taken at Paris's Opéra-Bastille, inaugurated in 1989 and regarded by some as a second storming of the Bastille. Just as the solid bourgeois of the 19th century replaced the aristocratic patrons of old, concrete and glass have now driven out stone and statuary, though without very much change to what happens on the stage inside. In the United States the opera house can be a skyscraper, in Mexico City a museum, in Cairo a palace out of *A Thousand and One Nights*, and in Seoul a galactic spiral. Other operatic venues are still under construction or reconstruction, some of them to return in the same cherished form they enjoyed before their accidental demise. Today opera prepares to enter the third millennium by casting its architecture, like its repertory, in the past but always freshly perfect tense.

Thierry Beauvert

I The Curtain Rises

Teatro Olimpico
Vicenza

1580. *Work begins, from plans by Andrea Palladio, on 28 February behind the harsh exterior of an old fortress. After the death of the architect on 19 August, Vincenzo Scamozzi takes charge of the project, which is generally based on Roman prototypes.*

1585. *Inaugurated on 3 March with one of the first attempts to revive Sophocles's* Oedipus the King *in Italian, complete with sung chorus.*

1653. *Maffei decorates the walls with narrative friezes and trompe-l'oeil effects.*

1750. *Cassetti adds a balustrade with posts serving as plinths for a line of statuary on top of the colonnade behind the hemicycle of fourteen tiered rows. The stage wall (*frons scenae*) is embellished, in the manner of a Roman triumphal arch, with columns, tabernacles, caryatids, and portrait sculptures of academicians, all arranged over two stories and an attic. Beyond the seven open doors piercing the* frons scenae, *lies Scamozzi's illusionistic décor of plunging perspectives representing streets lined into infinity with palaces, porticoes, temples, and arcades.*

A ndrea Palladio may be best known for his superb villas, those tokens of pride built by Venice's 16th-century patriciate and still scattered over the Italian countryside between Padua and Venice. In theatre design, however, Palladio was the all-important link between Classical antiquity—the great passion of early 17th-century Europe—and opera as it was then being brought to life in Florence. He had already built temporary wooden theatres in Vicenza, but in 1580 the Accademia Olimpica, of which he was himself a member, commissioned him to design a permanent venue for their productions of Classical drama. In the old fortress selected for its site, Palladio reinvented the classic Roman theatre, a form codified fifteen centuries earlier by Vitruvius, but he made the auditorium an ellipse instead of a hemicycle in order to accommodate a larger audience. Destiny, always ripe for tragedy, would deny Palladio the fruits of his work, which got under way only a few

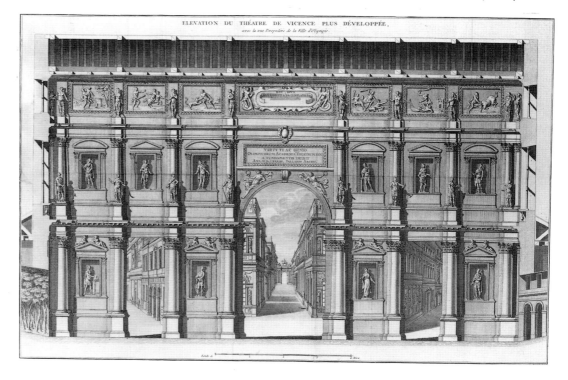

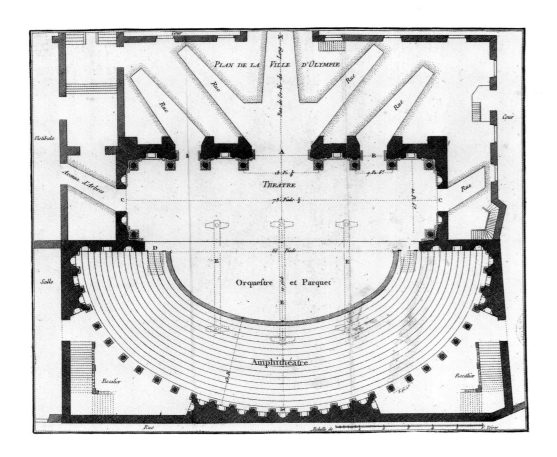

FACTS ABOUT THE BUILDING

1585 *Andrea Palladio, architect, succeeded by Vincenzo Scamozzi*
Capacity: 496
Fan-shaped auditorium
Proscenium: **width** 17.60m
Stage: **width** 24.60m; **height** 15m; **depth** 5.80m

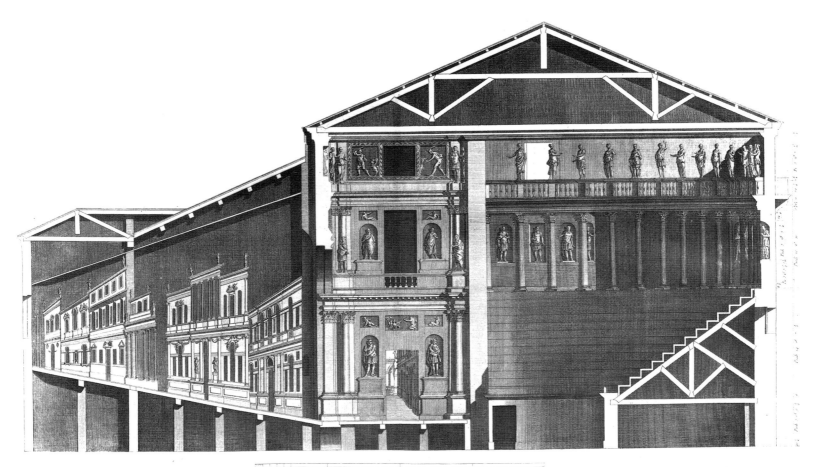

Gluck's *Iphigénie en Tauride:* scenery by Ezio Frigerio for the production by Luca Ronconi.

Jacopo Peri is generally credited with having composed the first true opera, a work of 1598 entitled Dafne. *He was also a singer admired at the Medici court and an active member of the Camerata of Florence, dedicated to the Renaissance project of re-endowing music with a noble purity comparable to that associated with Classical antiquity. The mythical origins of lyric art would appear indeed to lie with Orpheus, a theme that runs through Western music from Peri's* Euridice *to Milhaud's* Malheurs d'Orphée *(1925).* Euridice, *with a libretto by Ottavio Rinuccini, was performed in Florence on 6 October 1600 during celebrations honoring the marriage of Henri IV of France and Maria de' Medici. Peri himself sang the title role. The staging was by a nephew of Michelangelo Buonarroti, who displayed rare sophistication in his use of advanced machinery for each of the tableaux, thereby affirming the new* stile rappresentativo *or* monodico *of musical drama. This meant a monodic genre committed to textual clarity, simple, natural declamation with single, accompanied voices rather than the polyphony of earlier generations, and a score reflecting the expressive and poetic accents of the text itself.*

It is thought that Monteverdi attended the premiere of Euridice. *The work would soon inspire similar efforts by other composers. Monteverdi was working on an* Orfeo *as early as 1605, with a libretto by Striggio. Given in Mantua in 1606, it reconfirmed a theme so fundamental to opera that it would attract composers throughout the history of the medium.*

months before he died, leaving his disciple, Vincenzo Scamozzi, to complete the fixed scenery modelled on the antique world. For Sophocles's *Oedipus the King*, chosen by the Academy as a symbol of Classical renascence, Scamozzi played on the wonder still caused by mathematical perspective and reconstituted a great triumphal arch, which opened, like so many Theban gates, into a fan-like array of seven streets, all racing away into simulated depth past endless temple and palace façades. Gabrieli's choruses, which accompanied the play at the inauguration, would never be performed in a more beautiful setting. As guardians of this new heritage, Vicenza's academicians left the building untouched until 1750, when they placed a balustrade atop the colonnade and, for a Neoclassical touch, decorated it with a line of statues. Scamozzi, after the death of Palladio, took his expertise to the ideal city of Sabbioneta, near Cremona, and created another Teatro Olimpico, where, under ceilings frescoed in Veronese's style, all the magic of the Gonzagan era would crystallize. In 1628 Palladio's masterpiece gained one final descendant in the Teatro Farnese at Parma, where Aleotti stretched the Palladian plan until it became a horseshoe, creating an immense vessel capable of holding an audience of 4,500. In the arena thus formed equestrian displays and naval battles could be staged. But Palladian perfection may have received its most beautiful tribute four centuries later, when Ezio Frigerio reproduced the tiered rows of Palladio's Basilica at Vicenza as the setting for a production of Gluck's *Iphigénie en Tauride* sumptuously costumed *à l'antique* (above).

VIRTVTI AC GENIO
OLYMPICOR ACADEMIA THEATRVM HOC
A FVNDAMENTIS EREXIT
ANN MDLXXXIIII PALLADIO ARCHIT.

Grand-Théâtre
Bordeaux

GRAND-THÉÂTRE
Bordeaux - France

1773. *The Maréchal Duc de Richelieu commissions the Parisian architect Victor Louis to design the Grand-Théâtre.*

1780. *Inaugurated 7 April with Act I of Racine's* Athalie. *The first night is delayed because of the hostility of a group of local notables towards Victor Louis. Spaciously planned, the Grand-Théâtre stands clear on all four sides. It contains 1,158 seats. The decorative muses and goddesses on the colonnade of the main façade are by the sculptors Berruer and Vandendrix.*

GRAND THÉÂTRE DE BORDEAUX
FAÇADE LATÉRALE.

If the Grand-Théâtre in Bordeaux remains, even today, one of the architectural gems of France, it is because it was born of an encounter between two people of extraordinary will-power. The first of these was a Richelieu, the luxury-loving Governor of Guyenne and a grand-nephew of the illustrious Cardinal, who forced upon the inhabitants of Bordeaux an architect named Victor Louis, a man altogether worthy of his despotic patron. The cost was going to be colossal, but by 1780 the great theatre had risen proudly, like an act of defiance against Parisian power and the ideals of the approaching Revolution. For the first time a theatre was treated as an entirely freestanding public monument, the focus of every urban perspective, and it opened the way to a whole line of "cathedral theatres"—*théâtres basiliques*—the climax of which would come a century later in the Palais Garnier at the heart of Paris. As massive as a Greek temple, with a tall colonnade across the front and public arcades along the sides, the Grand-Théâtre represents an important break with tradition in several ways. Louis allowed the roof of the auditorium and the elevated stage "tower" to be visible above the attic balustrade. Although the roof is still made of wood, he reinforced the columns of the portico with iron. This technological advance looked forward to the metal structure the architect would employ a bit later for the Salle Montansier, the future home of the Comédie-Française in Paris.

Bordeaux saw itself as the second capital of France, and was used to thinking big. So was Victor Louis, who reserved as much space for the various foyers and circulation areas as for the auditorium and stage combined. He even treated the public spaces theatrically in their own right, dramatizing the Piranesian contrast between the cavernous vestibule and the luminous elegance of the grand staircase mounting to balconies

An armature of iron, anchored in the architrave and the façade wall, counteracts the enormous outward thrust of the flat vault against the freestanding corner columns. The technique would be known as "Louis' nail." On the lateral façades are 21 giant Corinthian pilasters and a covered pedestrian arcade.

1799. *The Grand-Théâtre is restored following damage suffered during the Revolution. It remains one of the few theatres in Europe never to have been consumed by flames.*

1806. *Financial difficulties force the administration to mine the saltpeter under a basement wall.*

1837. *The space above the vestibule to the 700-seat concert hall is transformed into a ballroom and then into a foyer.*

1853. *The Robin ceiling is restored and the theatre returned to its original form by Charles-Bernard Burguet, the city architect. William-Adolphe Bouguereau paints the ceiling of the foyer.*

1871. *The Third Republic is proclaimed in the Grand-Théâtre, which becomes the seat of the French parliament during the Prussian Siege of Paris.*

1880. *The centenary of Victor Louis' Grand-Théâtre is celebrated in the presence of Charles Garnier, architect of the Opéra in Paris.*

1915. *Restoration of the Robin ceiling, distempered directly on to wood. Charles Niquet installs machinery capable of raising the orchestra stalls level with the stage.*

1919, 1938, 1977. *Successive restorations.*

1990-1991. *The reception rooms, the auditorium, and the stage apparatus are all restored using the most up-to-date methods.*

FACTS ABOUT THE BUILDING

1780 *Victor Louis, architect*
1837 and 1853 *Charles-Bernard Burguet, architect*
1990-91 *Bernard Fanquernie, architect*
Capacity: 1,114
Bell-shaped auditorium
4 levels of balcony
Proscenium: **width** 11.80m; **height** 9m
Stage: **width** 24m; **depth** 16m

from which patrons could watch the fashionable spectacle below. All these things would become primary inspiration for Charles Garnier, who acknowledged his debt by attending the centenary celebration of the Grand-Théâtre. The acoustically superb auditorium, inscribed within a truncated circle flared like a bell towards the stage, is an improvement over the Italian model in its sight lines, shortening the distance between the stage and the most remote box. Finally, there is the stage, which Victor Louis equipped with the very latest technology.

Damaged by the Revolution but not set on fire, remodeled numerous times during the first half of the 19th century, and then "restored" in the Second Empire manner, the Grand-Théâtre would have to await the eve of its bicentenary before an exemplary restoration could give it back the classical beauty that it originally possessed. With this, it became evident that the great Bordeaux theatre was both the culmination of its type and the germ of innovations to come.

Although the Duc de Richelieu (a grand-nephew of the Cardinal), in his capacity as Governor of the Aquitaine, had commissioned the Grand-Théâtre, he did not attend the inauguration, marked by a performance of Racine's Athalie, a half-play/half-opera, set to music by Franz Beck. On the same day he married, at the age of 84!

During the 19th century a regular opera company performed an ambitious repertory, including Wagner's Götterdämmerung, Halévy's La Juive, and Meyerbeer's L'Africaine.

1969. *Premiere of Dussaut's* Altamina.

Premieres of foreign operas in French translation:

1894. *Leoncavallo's* I Pagliacci

1967. *Britten's* Gloriana.

Important revivals of older works:

1957. *Lully's* Armide.

1958. *Verdi's* Don Carlos.

Premieres of French works outside their original theatres:

1895. *Massenet's* La Navarraise.

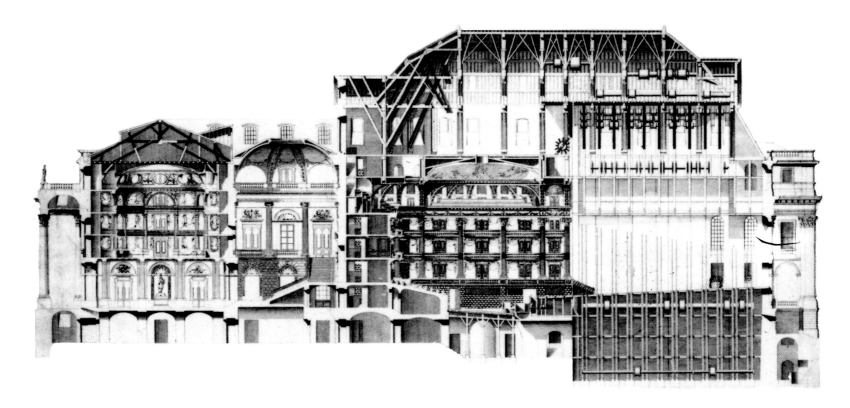

1950. *Bordeaux's "Mai musical" festival is inaugurated.*

The Bordeaux Opéra has long been the second most important opera house in France, after Paris. A new administration now fosters a program of regional co-production, undertaken mainly with the Capitole de Toulouse and the Théâtre d'Avignon, offering, for example, Puccini's Turandot *and* La Fanciulla del West, *Tchaikovsky's* Eugene Onegin, *and Verdi's* Nabucco. *The "Mai musical" constitutes a major event in the musical life of Bordeaux, over the years attracting such talents as Yehudi Menuhin, Alfred Cortot, Robert Casadesus, and Charles Munch. Bordeaux has thus frequently been the first French city to hear such foreign artists as Giacomo Lauri-Volpi, Kirsten Flagstad, Lauritz Melchior, Martti Talvela, Kiri Te Kanawa, Thomas Allen, and Samuel Ramey.*
1992. *The fully restored Grand-Théâtre is opened with a new production of Mozart's* The Magic Flute *designed by Roberto di Simone.*

L'Opéra-Théâtre
of Nicolas Ledoux

L'OPÉRA-THÉÂTRE OF NICOLAS LEDOUX
Besançon - France

1778. *Construction is begun to plans by Claude Nicolas Ledoux, and carried out under the supervision of the architect Claude Joseph Alexandre Bertrand. The theatre is one of the first ever to have orchestra stalls furnished with seats.*

1784. *Inaugurated on 9 August with Piron's* La Métromanie *and André Modest Grétry's* Le Tableau parlant *in the presence of Louis-Joseph de Bourbon, Prince de Condé.*

1836. *The theatre is restored, with a new ceiling by the painter Chazerand frescoed over Boquet's original decoration.*

1857. *A new restoration, undertaken by the architect Delacroix, removes the entrance steps, lowers the vestibule, installs a new foyer, and raises the first balcony.*

1958. *The theatre is ravaged by fire on 29 April, only to be rebuilt within four months by a team of three hundred workers. The new auditorium is inaugurated on November 20 with Verdi's* Otello. *The old façade survives, complete with its bluish-ochre limestone, its six Ionic columns and smooth entablature, its three entrance doors and high mansard roof.*

1994. *Ledoux's theatre is freshly restored and renamed the Opéra-Théâtre. Both foyer and auditorium are redecorated, the orchestra pit enlarged, and the entire*

It was thanks to revenues from the Salines Royales, or Royal Salt Works, of Franche-Comté, and to the faithful support of the intendant Charles André Lacoré, that Claude Nicolas Ledoux could realize at least part of his ideal city, Arc-et-Senans—the Théâtre de Besançon, a symbolic pendant to that unfinished microcosm, which opened on 9 August 1784 in the presence of the Prince de Condé. Steeped in Neoclassicism, Ledoux adopted the austere, dignified manner of a Greco-Roman temple for the exterior, an Ionic colonnade its sole embellishment, and a tall mansard roof dictated by the region's heavy snowfall. Within the building Ledoux was able freely to express his social and humanistic theories. As we know from the famous print entitled *Coup d'oeil sur le théâtre de Besançon* (overleaf), he combined natural principles and Roman traditions in a perfect hemicycle "so that everyone can see and be seen." A total of two thousand spectators sat in thirty-six regularly rising rows of seats. At the same time, Ledoux reversed the traditional order of things and decreed "that the one who pays the least should be the most distant." And so the stalls, the floor of the house, which had always been a "sheepfold" for standees and the place where cabals would begin, became one of the very first ground-floor sections in any theater to have seats and the cream of the audience to occupy them. The boxes, "those birdcages where perched the mighty of the earth," were made more respectable by having their partitions lowered to waist-level. The first section was reserved for the nobility, the second for the "honest bourgeoisie," and the third for "workers and shop girls." The lower classes found themselves relegated to the "gods". A "universal" harmony would, according to Ledoux, reign over the hemispherical form of the auditorium, the quality of whose acoustics the architect improved, long before Wagner, by sinking the orchestra pit and backing it with a concave baffle designed to project sound towards the audience. All eyes focused on the stage undistracted by décor, which consisted merely of a proscenium arch with illusionistic stonework and an overall color scheme of blue, gray, gold, and silver. Here too Besançon was far ahead of Bayreuth. Behind the scenes, Ledoux also proved visionary when he planned a back-stage area and spaces at the sides. Alas, the French Revolution, which exploded in 1789, had no sympathy for the utopias of the Ancien

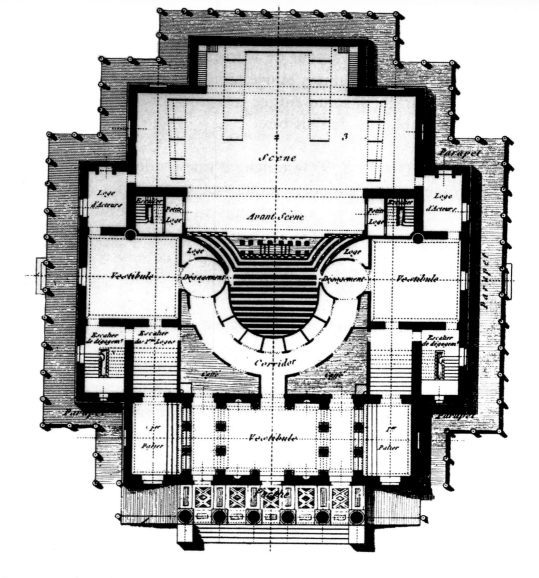

stage renovated to include the latest technology.

1995. *The renovated theatre opens on 11 January with a performance by the variety singer Claude Nougaro, son of the theatre's former director.*

1995-1996 season. *A repertory of ten classic operas includes Puccini's* Tosca, *Mozart's* Così Fan Tutte, *and Pouillard's* Le Jeune Werther, *as well as the novelty of three operas with libretti by Bertolt Brecht:* Der Ozeanflug, Der Jasager und der Neinsager *and* Das Badener Lehrstück von Einverständnis.

Engraving by Nicolas Ledoux showing the auditorium of the Besançon theatre inside a huge eye.

FACTS ABOUT THE BUILDING

1736-1806 *Claude Nicholas Ledoux, architect*
Capacity: 2,000
Bell-shaped auditorium
Proscenium: **width** 12m; **depth** 8m
Stage: **depth** 30m

Régime. By the end of the turmoil there was nothing behind Ledoux's façade but utter desolation. In 1836, however, the theatre recovered its chandelier, and Chazerand's new ceiling was placed over the original painting of Apollo and the Muses executed by Boquet, the painter of Versailles' *Menus-Plaisirs*. Twenty years later, the Chazerand canvas would be replaced by a regionalist work. The auditorium was updated by the architect Delacroix in the taste of the Second Empire, though he did not dare to touch the partitioned boxes. A century later, on the night of 29 April 1958, the theatre went up in flames, a catastrophe that so affected the people of Besançon that they immediately voted funds for its reconstruction, and indeed a few months later the familiar façade would once again grace the heart of the old city. But the colonnade had ceased to be anything more than a screen. Ledoux's utopian interior had disappeared. The Opera of the Enlightenment had become a historical document, leaving the new auditorium—itself reconstructed in 1994—to appease audiences with the comforts of modern technology.

Théâtre Graslin
Nantes

THÉÂTRE GRASLIN
Nantes - France

1776. The Nantes speculator Jean-Joseph Graslin commissions Mathurin Crucy, a pupil of Boullée, to design and build a theatre for the city.
1788. Work on the theatre is completed, together with the facing U-shaped plaza designed by Crucy as part of an overall, coordinated plan. Inaugurated on 23 March, Easter Sunday. We do not know the work performed.
1796. Fire destroys all but the essential fabric of the theatre.
1808. Reconstruction is begun, under the supervision of Crucy, the original architect.

Real-estate speculation, it appears, can sometimes serve the public good. In 1776 a citizen of Nantes called Jean-Joseph Graslin, who had made his money as a businessman and tax-collector, started upon a vast campaign of urban development. Having acquired Church property overlooking the port, he engaged Mathurin Crucy, the city building inspector, to design a new quarter whose centerpiece would be the theatre. A pupil of the visionary Neoclassicist Étienne-Louis Boullée, Crucy seized on the occasion to pay homage to the architectural purity of ancient Greece. With infinite care, he calculated the proportional relationship between the double colonnade of the façade and the plaza immediately in front, itself a U-shape mirroring that of the auditorium within. This interplay between interior and exterior continues in the coffer-vaulted foyer, the sort of deep Piranesian space in which spectators can no longer tell whether they are inside or out, since the actual theatre starts only on the other side of a wall at the top of stairs leading up to the promenade around the boxes. The auditorium, an intimate hall with a traditional shape and a flat ceiling, was modeled on a theatre designed by Jacques-Germain Soufflot at Lyons with bell-shaped balconies and a top gallery. Eight years after its completion in 1788, Crucy's opera house was swept by fire, which broke out during a performance of Grétry's *Zémire et Azore* and consumed everything but the structural fabric. Only in 1808 would reconstruction commence, under Crucy himself, thanks to a visit by Napoleon and a decree granting the city a measure of financial aid. In the meantime, the architect had tried his hand at naval architecture, which gave him the idea for a low-pitched roof invisible from the outside. This time Crucy took the precaution of building a cistern for use

1813. Reopened after rebuilding on 3 May, with a one-act prologue in verse entitled Molière à la nouvelle salle, *written for the reopening of the Odéon in Paris and adapted for Nantes. This was followed by a three-act opera, André Modeste Grétry's* Aline ou la reine de Golgonde, *in a production designed by Crucy, who had already decorated the Salon de Molière.*

1838. Lighting is improved with the introduction of gas.

1865. The auditorium is redecorated in red and gold.

1880. The auditorium, foyers, and stage boxes are all restored, and a new chandelier hung from the auditorium ceiling.

1881. A ceiling painted by Hippolyte Berteaux replaces the classical coffering.

1887. Measures are taken to fire-proof the theatre.

1895. The floor of the orchestra pit is lowered by 80cm.

1912. Electric lighting is updated.

1956. The vestibule is renovated.

1968. The theatre restored close to its original state.

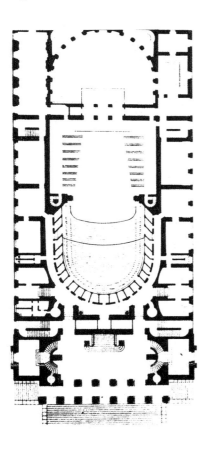

Detail of the ceiling painting by Hippolyte Berteaux.

in the event of another fire; he also redesigned the orchestra stalls on a ramp, redecorated the auditorium in soft colors, embellished the curtain with Napoleonic bees, and introduced stage machinery comparable to that at the Odéon in Paris. By 1813 the Théâtre Graslin was ready to resume its career. In 1825 statues of eight muses were placed above the portico, but the typical piece of academic painting on the ceiling—a work of 1881—is an unmistakable legacy of the Third Republic. Time then stopped for the little opera house until 1968, when restoration left the auditorium refreshed in the original spirit of Crucy. This campaign was followed a decade later by another one designed to overhaul and update the stage machinery.

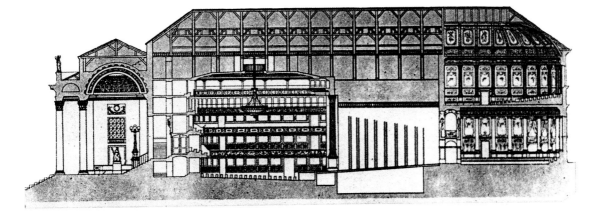

Auditorium of the Théâtre Graslin at Nantes at the time of Louis Philippe. The two columns on each side of the stage have now disappeared.

FACTS ABOUT THE BUILDING

1788 and **1814** *Mathurin Crucy, architect*
Fan-shaped auditorium
Capacity: 970
Sloping orchestra stalls
4 balconies
1 gallery
Proscenium: **width** 10m; **height** 7m
Stage: width 17m; **height** 16m; **depth** 15m

Gran Teatro La Fenice *Venice*

1789. *The* nobile società *launches a competition for a new theatre in opera's beacon city. Gianantonio Selva wins the commission over twenty-eight other contestants.*

1792. *La Fenice is Venice's first Neoclassical building. It rose along a new canal into which numerous pilings had been driven to secure the foundation. On the canal side an arcaded portico (below) opens directly from the quay into the backstage area. On the* campo *side, Giovanni Ferrari's*

It was in Venice that the first commercial theatre opened its doors, in 1637, and it was here, a few years later, that the engineer Torelli perfected his amazing "machines." Again, it was in the lagoon city, during the year 1642, that Carlo Fontana introduced the horseshoe auditorium, a form that soon became standard in theatrical architecture. It was here, too, in the mid-18th century, that the custom started of lowering the curtain between acts. At the end of the previous century Venice could boast no less than 16 active theatres, and in 1701 some 365 new works were performed on Venetian stages. Such was the context, in the years prior to the fall of the Republic, for the birth of La Fenice (the Phoenix). It was so called because it rose from the ashes of the Teatro San Benedetto, Venice's leading opera house, destroyed by fire in 1774. After this disaster, wealthy opera lovers decided to treat themselves to the most beautiful of all theatres. They therefore launched a carefully defined competition, won by Gianantonio Selva, who proposed a Neoclassical building facing on one side a *campo*, or small plaza, and on the other a canal, excavated at the architect's behest so that spectators could gain immediate access via the backstage area. In the auditorium—its gilded décor overlaid with a blue less gaudy than the purple that came later—a total of 170 identical boxes rose in tiers completely round the horseshoe. The Imperial box arrived only in 1808, on the eve of a visit from Napoleon. In 1836 the theatre was completely destroyed by fire. Rebuilding began immediately, under two architect brothers, Tommaso and Giambattista Meduna. Within a year, the Phoenix had sprung up anew but in a form consistent with the original design by Gianantonio Selva. In the 19th century La Fenice became a mecca for singers, despite the demanding Venetian public, helping to establish the fame first of Rossini and then

statues representing Melpomene and Terpsichore adorn the façade. Francesco Fontanesi is responsible for the decoration of the auditorium. Inaugurated 16 May with Paisiello's I Giuocchi d'Agrigento.

1808. *The auditorium is redecorated by Giuseppe Borsato.*

1836. *The auditorium is completely destroyed by fire, whereupon the brothers Meduna reconstruct it basically following Selva's original plans. Transquillo Orsi paints the ceiling as a trompe-l'oeil pergola, while Sebastiano Santi decorates the hall in the Empire style.*

1837. *The rebuilt Fenice is inaugurated 26 December.*

1848. *The Imperial box is destroyed anew during the revolution. A year later the Austrian overlords have it rebuilt and redecorated, again by Meduna and Borsato.*

1854. *The Meduna brothers redecorate again, this time in the Rococo manner.*

1878. *Cadorin modernizes the stage.*

1937. *Three centuries after the world's first public theatre opened in Venice, the* nobile società *cedes La Fenice to the city. The engineer Eugenio Miozzi installs modern machinery, including a revolving stage, while working with Nino Barbantini to restore the décor in a manner consistent with the original.*

1976. *The Dante Salon on the piano nobile is redecorated with frescoes painted by Virgilio Guidi.*

1996. *On 29 January, during a campaign of renovation, fire broke out and quickly spread, in part because water had been drained from nearby canals for maintenance reasons. The municipality cut aesthetic quarrels short by quickly announcing that La Fenice would be rebuilt, before the end of the millennium, in a form identical to the one designed by Selva in 1789-1792 and decorated by the Meduna brothers in 1854.*

FACTS ABOUT THE BUILDING

1792 *Gianantonio Selva, architect*
1837 *Tommaso and Giambattista Meduna, architects*
1937 *Eugenio Miozzi, architect, engineer, and decorator*
Capacity: 1,500
Horseshoe auditorium
3 tiers of boxes
2 galleries
Proscenium: **width** 13.40m; **height** 8m
Stage: **width** 21.80m; **height** 24m; **depth** 33m

Giuseppe Verdi, by Boldoni.

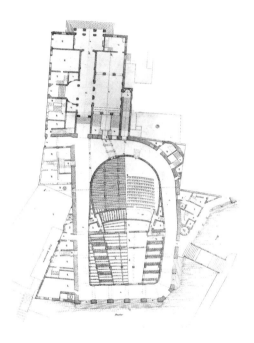

of Verdi. These prudent composers took care to adapt their works to the legendary mediocrity of the Venetian chorus and orchestra, none of which saved *Rigoletto* and *Traviata* from the booing that erupted during their premieres at La Fenice. As for the theatre itself, Venetians have never wavered in their love. On 29 January 1996, unkind fate struck again; once more fire gutted La Fenice, leaving only the façade and four walls. But the phoenix, true to its legend, will rise from the ashes, splendid as ever, in time for the dawn of the new millennium.

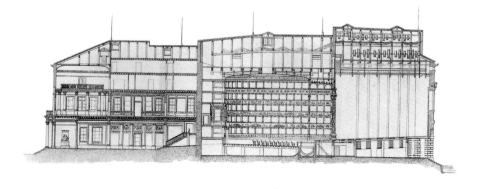

Scene from *Senso*, a film by Luchino Visconti, set in La Fenice, Venice.

Opera houses have sometimes been the setting for important films, such as Luchino Visconti's Senso *(1954), whose 19th-century drama of tragic love, between a young Austrian officer and the Countess Livia, unfolds partly at La Fenice during Austria's occupation of the Veneto. This romantic tale begins in the course of a performance of* Il Trovatore, *at a time when Venice is under attack from the Austrian and Italian armies. The songs taken up by the Italian soldiers are arias from Verdi operas, and the volatile throng in La Fenice's upper galleries, moved by the stentorian music of* Il Trovatore, *surges forward tossing down leaflets and flowers. The scene may very well have been inspired by the thunderous ovation given to Verdi at a Milanese performance of* Nabucco, *an opera in which the Babylonian captivity of the Jews reminded the audience of the misery endured by an Italy still in thrall to foreign powers.*

Important world premieres at La Fenice:
Cimarosa's Gli Orazi ed i Curiazi *(1796).*
Meyerbeer's Il Crociato in Egitto *(1824).*
Bellini's I Capuleti e i Montecchi *(1830) and* Beatrice di Tenda *(1833)*
Rossini's Tancredi *(1813) and* Semiramide *(1823).*
Donizetti's Belisario *(1836) and* Maria di Rudenz *(1838).*
Verdi's Ernani *(1844),* Attila *(1846),* Rigoletto *(1851),* La Traviata *(1853), and* Simon Boccanegra *(1857)*
Stravinsky's The Rake's Progress *(1951)*
Benjamin Britten's The Turn of the Screw *(1954).*
Nono's Intolleranza *(1961).*

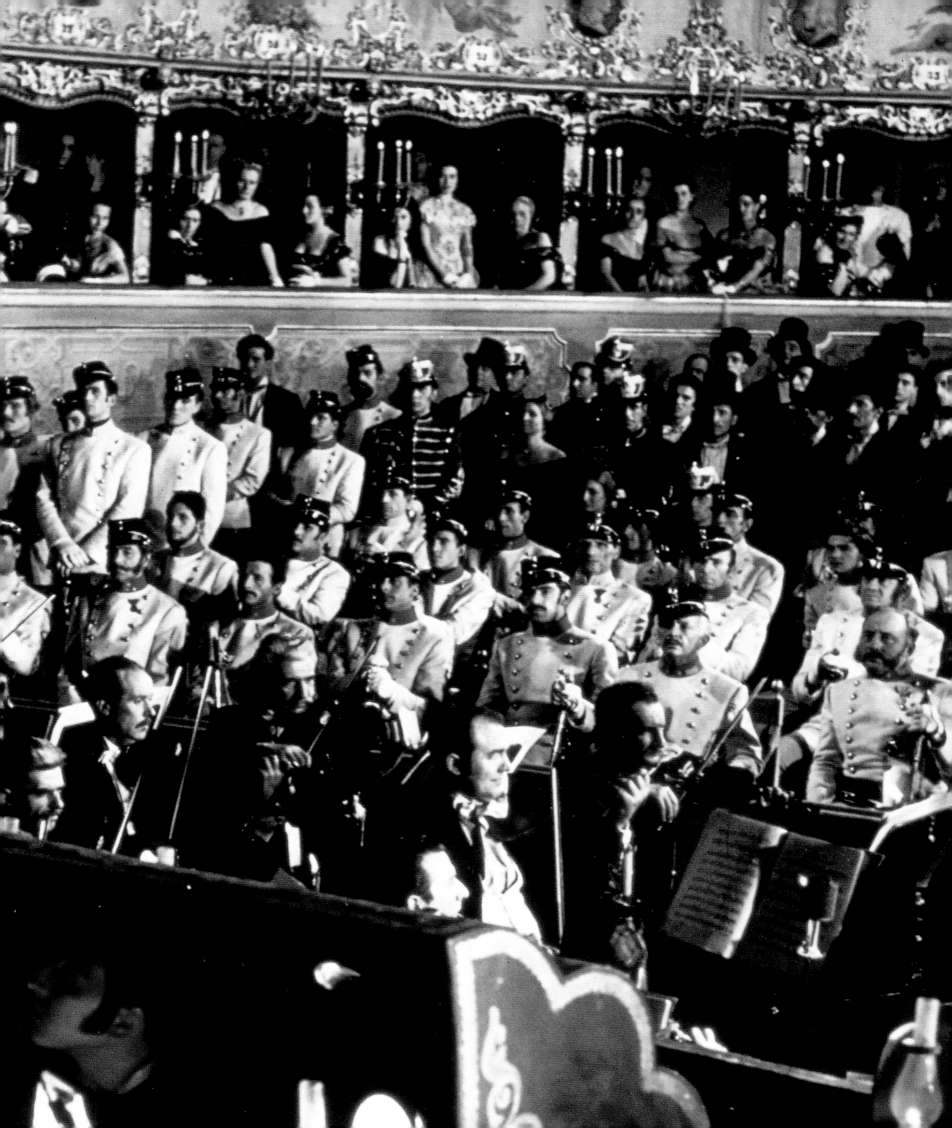

II Court Architecture

Teatro di
San Carlo Naples

1734. *Charles III de Bourbon, viceroy of Naples and Sicily, commissions a new theatre from the architects Giovanni Antonio Medrano and Angelo Carasale.*

Renata Tebaldi.

The original Teatro di San Carlo was built to replace the old Teatro San Bartolomeo, which had become too small for the city's needs. It was a temple dedicated to *opera seria*, then all the rage in Naples. When completed in 1737, the San Carlo was indeed the most beautiful as well as the biggest opera house in the world, a status it would retain for many years to come. Equally important, its magnificence offered a potent symbol of Bourbon power, which held sway over the Two Sicilies even though somewhat curbed by Habsburg Austria. This explains why the 184 boxes tiered about the horseshoe remained without curtains, so that no one could avoid scrutiny by the sovereign, who could reach the San Carlo through a corridor linked to the royal palace. The architects, Giovanni Antonio Medrano and Angelo Carasale, took less than a year to construct their enormous theatre situated at the very center of Naples. But in 1808 Naples was conquered by the French and Napoleon made his greatest marshal, Joachim Murat, king. Shortly thereafter Murat commissioned a new façade for the San Carlo from one of the principal stage designers, Antonio Niccolini. His aim was to free the theatre from its courtly associations and assert its autonomy. His monumental front consisted of a massive, heavily rusticated lower story containing a public arcade and a colonnaded upper loggia crowned by a pediment embellished with a relief representing Parthenope, ancient Naples. Behind the colonnade lay the grand foyer. On 12 February 1816, at the height of Rossini's Neapolitan triumph, a roaring fire swept through the San Carlo Opera, destroying all but the new façade. Hardly had Ferdinand I de Bourbon recovered his throne, after the fall of Napoleon, when he ordered Niccolini to rebuild the theatre. The auditorium was enlarged to a total capacity of 3,500, but, obsessed by the danger of fire, the architect increased access routes and the number of stairways leading to and from it. Eleven months after the disaster, Naples's opera lovers, including the

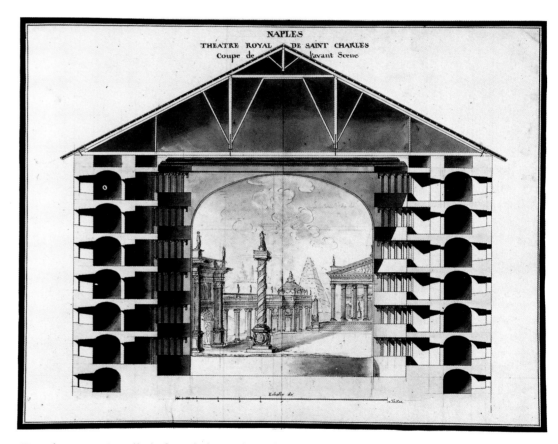

FACTS ABOUT THE BUILDING

1737 *Giovanni Antonio Medrano and Angelo Carasale, architects*
1810 *Antonio Niccolini, architect*
Horseshoe auditorium
Capacity: 1,444
Stage: **width** 33.50m; **depth** 34.50m; **height** 30m

French writer Stendhal, found themselves rhapsodizing over the new auditorium, its boxes draped in blue and its soft, bronze-toned ceiling fresco dedicated to Apollo. Only in 1854 did today's red and gold color scheme become a permanent feature of the San Carlo, by which time the theatre had been overtaken by La Scala in Milan as Italy's premier opera house. In 1870 the orchestra pit was rebuilt, at the recommendation of Giuseppe Verdi, and in 1890 the magic of electricity arrived, at a time when the city's teeming poor could barely afford a single candle each. In the 1930s, the stage was modernized, and the foyer rehabilitated in a sumptuous manner. Finally, in 1946, the British repaired the bomb damage wrought upon a theatre that remains the pride of Southern Italy.

1815. *Rossini appointed musical director. His forceful personality leaves an indelible mark on the independent and vociferous Neapolitan public, which, in the 20th century, would vote Renata Tebaldi superior to Maria Callas. Premiere on 4 October of Giaochino Rossini's* Elisabetta regina d'Inghilterra. *A sold-out house was assured once the public learned that the cast would include Isabella Colbran, for whom Rossini wrote the whole of his Neapolitan œuvre. The names of both singer and composer were to be forever linked with that of the San Carlo Opera. Rossini and his diva were married in 1822. Naples's opera house holds the record for world premieres, having staged almost 450 of them. The birth of Neapolitan opera, in the works of Porpora, Hasse, Paisiello, Piccinni, and Cimarosa, matured into the reign of Rossini, who wrote eight full-length pieces for Naples. Thereafter came Donizetti, who remains as popular in Naples as Bellini and Verdi.*

Auditorium of the Teatro di San Carlo before 1816, by Michele Fossini.

Isabella Colbran *(1785-1845), a singer of Spanish origin, who began as a contralto, developed into a soprano, and triumphed as the unrivaled prima donna of her generation. Remarkable in tragic roles, she commanded a voice with a range of over three octaves.*

Ball at the Teatro di San Carlo, Naples.

Slottsteater Drottningholm and Kungliga Teatern Stockholm

SLOTTSTEATER
Drottningholm - Sweden

1754. *The first theatre built at Drottningholm Castle, a royal residence.*

1762. *The court theatre destroyed by fire.*

1764. *Architect Carl Frederik Adelcrantz is commissioned to erect a second theatre.*

1766. *Inaugurated on 25 July.*

1921. *Forgotten for more than a century, the theatre is rediscovered intact, complete with its stage machinery, which would be preserved.*

1922. *Inaugurated a second time, marking the 150th anniversary of Gustavus III's national revolution.*

For many people, Drottningholm conjures up the radiant face of a child listening to the opening bars of Mozart's *The Magic Flute* in the film by Ingmar Bergman. Time has not been kind to old wood-built theatres, but the little court opera in Sweden survives as a kind of modern miracle, a mirage transporting us back to the mid-18th century. It was built for Queen Lovisa Ulrika, consort of King Adolphus Frederick and the sister of Prussia's Frederick the Great, who wanted a theatre at her summer residence where she could enjoy the pleasures of French tragedy and Italian opera. Destroyed by fire in 1762, it was reconstructed four years later from the plans of Carl Frederik Adelcrantz, who created a veritable jewel box wrapped in a plain masonry shell. The design, for all its freshness and charm, had been tested by the same architect a few years earlier in the intimate world of Confidencen near Ulriksdal. The whole of Drottningholm's ochre-toned auditorium is oriented about the royal box placed directly facing the stage and furnished with a pair of Louis XV fauteuils. For once royalty had the best seats. The court, when admitted, sat farther back, on benches in the orchestra stalls or in the few side boxes, some of which retain the grille designed to assure anonymity. Drottningholm, the cradle of Swedish theatre, came into its glory in the 1780s during the reign of Gustavus III, the hero of Verdi's *Un Ballo in Maschera*. In 1791, shortly before his assassination, the King decided to supplement the little theatre with a salon in which to receive the performing artists. For this he engaged the services of the French-born and -trained Jean-Louis Desprez, who built the King's salon on the park side of the tiny opera house. At the same time, Gustavus also had the esplanade outside renovated as an open-air theatre where sumptuous costume parties would be held, evoking the magic of the Italian Renaissance. Then, as in a tale by Hans Christian Anderson, the Drottningholm theatre fell asleep and slumbered for more than a century, until a retainer at the Royal Library rediscovered it in 1921. Still intact were the original stage machinery and even the sets for some thirty productions, all ready to be rehung and dropped to re-create their illusionistic perspectives on a stage which

Scene from *The Magic Flute*, Ingmar Bergman's film in which the theatre of Drottningholm was reconstructed in the studio.

is a full-scale mirror image of the auditorium itself. In the years that followed, the 454-seat theatre, now sensitively restored, became once again a venue for summer productions. True to the spirit of Gustavus III, a librettist in his own right, the repertory is performed in Swedish and drawn entirely from the second half of the 18th century, the era of Handel, Mozart, Gluck, and Grétry. Even today, those who enter Drottningholm find themselves leaving the 20th century for a Rococo world tempered by the North, where, through the enchantment of period productions, modern audiences can return to the Age of Enlightenment. In this setting, where even the musicians in the orchestra pit wear satin clothes and powdered wigs, we ourselves are alone incongruous.

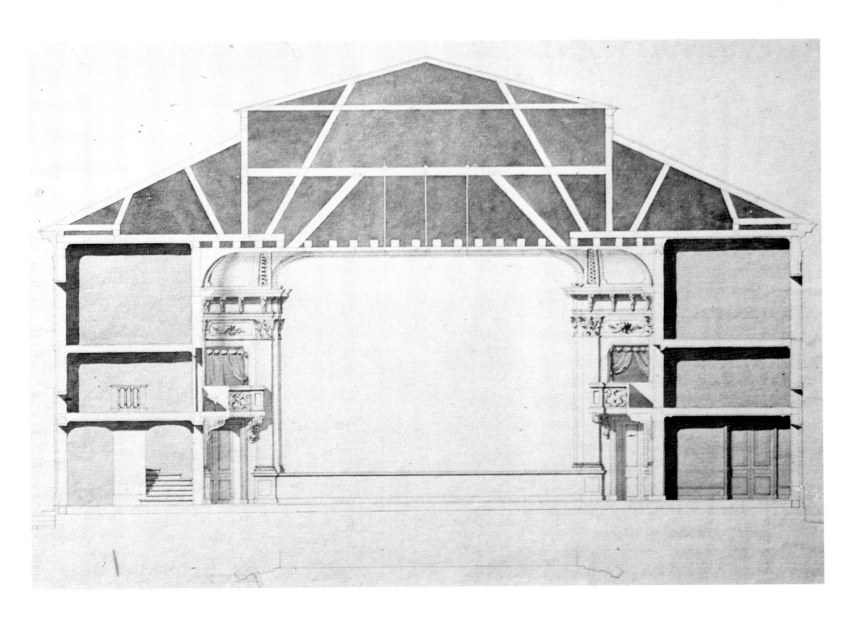

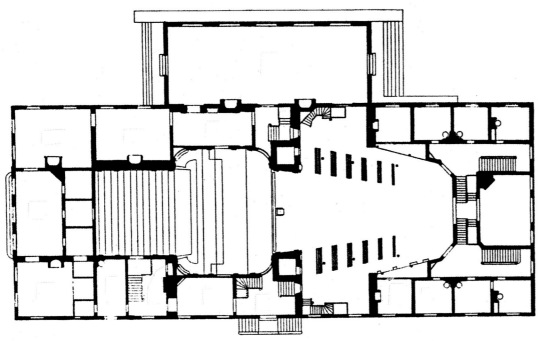

**FACTS ABOUT THE BUILDING:
SLOTTSTEATER**

1766 *Carl Frederik Adelcrantz, architect*
1791 *Jean-Louis Desprez, designer of the enlarged foyer*
Capacity: 454
Proscenium: **width** 8.80m; **heigh** 6.60m
Stage: **depth** 19.80m

**FACTS ABOUT THE BUILDING:
KUNGLIGA TEATERN**

1782 *Carl Frederik Adelcrantz, architect*
1898 *Axel Anderberg, architect*
Capacity: 1,200
Stage: **width** 11.25m; **depth** 18,25m; **height** 12.25m

KUNGLIGA TEATERN
Stockholm - Sweden

1782. *Commissioned by Gustavus III, the first Royal Opera in Stockholm is inaugurated. The Kungliga Teatern, a masterpiece designed by Adelcrantz, would be demolished in 1890.*

1898. *The new Royal Opera, designed by Axel Anderberg, is inaugurated with Franz Berwald's* Estrella de Soria.

The 19th century saw the arrival of the first Swedish operas, especially those composed by Franz Berwald.

1907. *Wagner's* Ring Cycle *is performed in Sweden for the first time, marking the start of a tradition in which many of the greatest Wagnerian singers would come from Scandinavia.*

1958. *An historically accurate production of Verdi's* Un Ballo in Maschera *is mounted, using the original libretto, with the court of Gustavus III as its setting and the assassination of the King as its climactic moment.*

1973. *The premiere of Werle's* Tintomara *marks the 200th anniversary of the founding of the first Swedish opera troupe, which performed in the Bohlhus (ballroom).*

1975. *Ingmar Bergman releases* The Magic Flute, *one of the most successful of all films based on opera. As his setting for the Mozart masterpiece, Bergman fashioned a scrupulously accurate reproduction of the Drottningholm court theatre, down to its machinery and its boxes. By using Drottningholm as décor he clearly anchored the fable to the stage of a real theatre, while still conveying a sense of enchantment and fantasy. Mozart's overture provides an excuse for exploring the theatre, where the faces of the audience display the same air of expectation.*

Right: Slottsteater, Drottningholm
Opposite: Kungliga Teatern, Stockholm

Théâtre de la Reine
Versailles

1779. *Inauguration of the theatre commissioned by Marie-Antoinette for the Petit Trianon and planned by Richard Mique.*

The stage-struck Queen performed the roles of Jenny in Sedaine's Le Roi et le fermier, *Agathe in* Le Sorcier de Poinsiniet, *and Colette in Jean-Jacques Rousseau's* Le Devin du village. La Gageure imprévue, *another work by Sedaine, and Barthe's* On ne s'avise jamais de tout *also came to life on the stage of this little court theatre, for the pleasure of an audience that could not resist declaring that the performances had been "royally bad." Today the auditorium is closed to the public, and its one hundred seats may be occupied only at the discretion of the President of the Republic.*

For Queen Marie-Antoinette, music was more than a distraction, it was an art known to her from her childhood in Vienna, where she had practiced under the tuition of Christoph Willibald von Gluck. Bored with her role as the consort of Louis XVI, and weary of both harp and harpsichord, Marie-Antoinette decided to take up singing again, but not at the Royal Opera, a bastion of the court etiquette she fled on every possible occasion. What she wanted was a little theatre of her own near the Petit Trianon, an exquisite 18th-century mansion built for Louis XV in the great park at Versailles by Ange-Jacques Gabriel. For the latest royal caprice, the fragile finances of pre-Revolutionary France would somehow be made to stretch a bit further. Early in 1779, the twenty-four-year-old Queen dispatched Richard Mique, her faithful architect, to copy the plans for the theatre at Choisy-le-Roi, which were then adapted to the Versailles site, where the new theatre would be inaugurated in July. The tiny blue and gold auditorium glittered with a gem-like beauty even though its pilasters were of stucco and its reliefs of papier-mâché. The stage machinery, devised by Boullet, was not only fully functional but also quite sophisticated. At last Marie-Antoinette could revel in her favorite pastime, performing in such ballad operas as Rousseau's *Le Devin de village* and Sedaine's *Le Roi et le fermier*, before an audience of intimates and servants, the latter secluded behind grillework screens. The Queen even organized a "Company of Nobles," some of whom were members of the royal family. Ten years later, with pastorales well out of fashion, French Revolutionaries sold the heavy velvet curtain for three hundred *livres*. After the Terror, Napoleon felt free to restore the little theatre for Marie-Louise, the Austrian niece of Marie-Antoinette who had become his second Empress. During the reign of Louis-Philippe (1830-48), royal blue gave way to bourgeois crimson and would not return until after 1950, when a new restoration allowed Gabriel's toy opera house once again to breathe the perfumed air of the Ancien Régime. With its stage set for Lully's *Thésée*, the theatre offers an Ariadne thread by which the late 20th century may wind its way through the maze of time to the carefree palace of Marie-Antoinette.

Opéra Royal Versailles

OPÉRA ROYAL
Versailles - France

*I*f your christian name is Angel you can be on familiar terms with the gods. Certainly Ange-Jacques Gabriel must have been when he began studying the theatre arts in preparation for the masterpiece he built at Versailles, a work that would prove enormously influential. In 1770, as the wedding of the Dauphin to Marie-Antoinette approached, Louis XV suddenly began worrying that the royal château possessed no proper theatre. Louis XIV, the Sun King and builder of Versailles, had in fact commissioned Mansart to erect an auditorium, but a burgeoning court soon required that the space be carved up into additional apartments. Meanwhile, the dithering monarchy kept Gabriel, appointed in 1748, waiting some fifteen years, before allowing him to start work on the new theatre. He took over the Mansart site, harmonized his façades with those already standing, and on the interior constructed an elliptical auditorium, a form much favored in Italy at the time. Then, through a clever interplay of mirrors, columns, and balconies, Gabriel created the effect of considerable grandeur despite the intimacy of the setting. Also illusory is the Rococo avalanche of marble and gilt, since the whole thing is fashioned in wood, from the ceiling down to the most delicate relief work. Thanks to its sophisticated machinery, this palace of mirages could be transformed in two hours into a grand ballroom, while the stage was the largest in the kingdom, a primacy that endured for almost a century. Plundered during the Revolution, repainted by Frédéric Nepveu in the lavish taste of Louis-Philippe, equipped with gaslight by Napoleon III, and taken over by the Senate of the Third Republic, Gabriel's beautiful opera house would not recover its integrity—the state it enjoyed when built for the marriage of the future Louis XVI—until 1957, following five years of almost archaeological investigation, which, for once, endowed the term "restoration" with its true patents of nobility.

FACTS ABOUT THE BUILDING

1769 Jacques Ange Gabriel, architect
capacity: 712
Elliptical auditorium
Proscenium: **width** 32,77m
Stage: **width** 32,80m; **height** 18m; **depth** 29m

The Bolshoi Theatre *Moscow*

THE BOLSHOI THEATRE
Moscow - Russia

1780. *The Petrovsky—the first Bolshoi Theatre—is built by Prince Pyotor Urusov and the rich English merchant Michael Maddox.*

1825. *The Bolshoi is inaugurated on 7 January with* The Triumph of the Muses, *a dance pantomime, following destruction by fire and then reconstruction by Ossip Bove from plans by Andrei Mikhailov.*

1856. *A new fire, followed by reconstruction under the supervision of architect Alberto Cavos. The new theatre is inaugurated on 20 August with Bellini's* I Puritani. *The portico on the main façade boasts eight colossal columns supporting a wide pediment crowned with a bronze quadriga driven by the god Apollo. The immense saddle-back roof covers a horseshoe auditorium with a capacity of 2,000 seats and a stage measuring some 80-metres deep. The two-story imperial box opens at the back onto a truly imperial foyer, transformed into the Beethoven Concert Hall in 1922.*

1942. *The Bolshoi is repaired after war damage.*

While most nations have now learned to treasure their architectural heritage, Russia seems indifferent to the fate of one of its most beautiful opera houses, a theatre that survived both the Romanovs and the Revolution only to suffer the cruellest kind of neglect under the post-Soviet regime. Its problems range from water-logged foundations to obsolete wiring. In fact the Bolshoi is in such a desperate state that UNESCO has been moved to raise the money necessary for essential repairs. Long gone are the ceremonial of Glinka's *A Life for the Tsar*, the pomp of Moussorgsky's *Boris*, and the splendour of Tchaikovsky's *The Queen of Spades*. The first Bolshoi—that is, the "Big Theatre" as opposed to the Maly or "Little Theatre"—was built in 1825 by Ossip Bove from the plans of Andrei Mikhailov. Its predecessor, the Petrovsky, had opened in 1780 and stood for a quarter of a century before succumbing to fire. The grandiose new house, with the tsar's consent, succeeded in putting the private theatres of the Moscow aristocracy out of business; it even rivaled the stages frequented by the court at their new capital, St. Petersburg. In 1853, a devastating fire left the Bolshoi with nothing but its outer shell, including the Neoclassical portico. Its reconstruction was completed three years later under the supervision of Alberto Cavos, the son of a Venetian composer who had settled in Russia. Cavos would also achieve fame as the architect of the rebuilt Maryinsky Theatre in St. Petersburg. (He was the grandfather of the stage designer Alexander Benois.) For the Bolshoi,

he salvaged pilasters and colonnades to create a classical temple, its main pediment crowned with a bronze quadriga driven by the god Apollo. For the purple and gold auditorium Cavos combined a horseshoe plan with a fan-like arrangement of seats in the

Catherine the Great (1729-1796) vigorously encouraged the development of opera in Russia, offering composers and performers the most generous fees then available at the courts of Europe. She even wrote libretti, in both Russian and French, most of them with a political theme: Fevey (1786), set to music by Pachkevich, and The Early Reign of Oleg (1786). Moscow took as it mission the discovery and advancement of Russian works, in contrast to the cosmopolitanism of St. Petersburg.
1880. Alexander III abolishes the aristocracy's exclusive access to the Bolshoi.

The royal box of the Bolshoi Theatre.

FACTS ABOUT THE BUILDING

1825 *Ossip Bove and Andrei Mikhailov, architects*
1856 *Alberto Cavos, architect*

Horseshoe auditorium
Capacity: 2,150
1 amphitheatre under the first balcony
4 balconies
1 top gallery
Proscenium: **width** 18-20m; **height** 11-15m
Stage: **width** 39.40m; **depth** 23-80m; **height** 30m

orchestra stalls. Also composite are the boxes, open to each other at the front in the French manner and enclosed at the back in the Italian tradition. Finally, if the circulation spaces were less than majestic, the foyer outside the imperial box was so vast that in the 1920s the Soviet authorities had it transformed into a concert hall. War-damaged in 1942, the Bolshoi once again underwent restoration, this time without any alteration, but no further improvements have been made during all the years since. If this great house entered history as the place where Rimsky-Korsakov, Chaliapin, and Stanislavsky won renown, its strategic location also made it a witness to a still larger history. Immediately in front of the entrance colonnade was where the Red Guards massed in 1917 prior to their assault on the Kremlin. In 1922 the Union of the Soviet Socialist Republics was proclaimed from the stage of the Bolshoi. Moreover, it was in the auditorium that the national electrification plan was adopted, the ultimate irony for a theatre now left in a chronic state of disrepair.

Nicolai Ghiaurov in Moussorgsky's
Boris Godunov.

The Maryinsky Theatre
St.Petersburg

P eter the Great founded his capital on the Gulf of Finland as a shining symbol of modern Russia, in contrast to the backwardness of Moscow. St. Petersburg opened its doors wide to Western culture, including opera—French, German, and Italian—which must have found it virtually on occupied territory. The first performances, beginning in 1723, took place in a wood-built theatre at the corner of the Nevsky Prospect, then at the imperial residence, and, after 1737, in the Winter Palace built by Bartolommeo Rastrelli. During the reign of Catherine II (1762-96), a devout Francophile, opera loomed still larger in Russia, thanks to the establishment of numerous private theatres. It spread further in the 1780s after the St. Petersburg Bolshoi opened, followed by a sumptuous theatre in the Hermitage next to the Winter Palace, and finally the Maly, or "Little Theatre," a venue accessible to everyone. French and Italian works appeared on these stages in rapid succession, usually very soon after their premieres in the West. In 1832, Nicholas I dedicated Rossi's Alexandrinsky Theatre to the Tsarina; four years later he ordered the rebuilding of the Bolshoi. It was inaugurated with Glinka's *A Life for the Tsar*, a work which thereafter would traditionally open the season, right up to the 1917 Revolution. Russian opera soon came to the fore, beginning at the turn of the 19th century when Tsar Paul I prohibited Italians from performing in Russia. Indeed, it was given its own theatre, the Circus, erected in 1855, burnt down in 1859, and rebuilt by Alberto Cavos, who had just resurrected Moscow's Bolshoi from the ashes. The new house also resembled an antique temple, complete with colonnaded portico and pediment, as well as a hipped roof. On the interior, moreover, Calvos opted for a gilded auditorium designed to enhance the theatricality of the imperial loge, surrounded by 1,600 seats distributed mainly along five tiers of boxes open at the sides in the French manner. Now the theatre would be known as the Maryinsky, remaining loyal to the Russian repertory, in contrast to the Mikhailovsky, another Cavos restoration, which favored French and Italian works. In 1890 the splendor of the Maryinsky was briefly threatened by an ambitious project cooked up in the mind of Victor Schroeter, who, inspired by Semper in

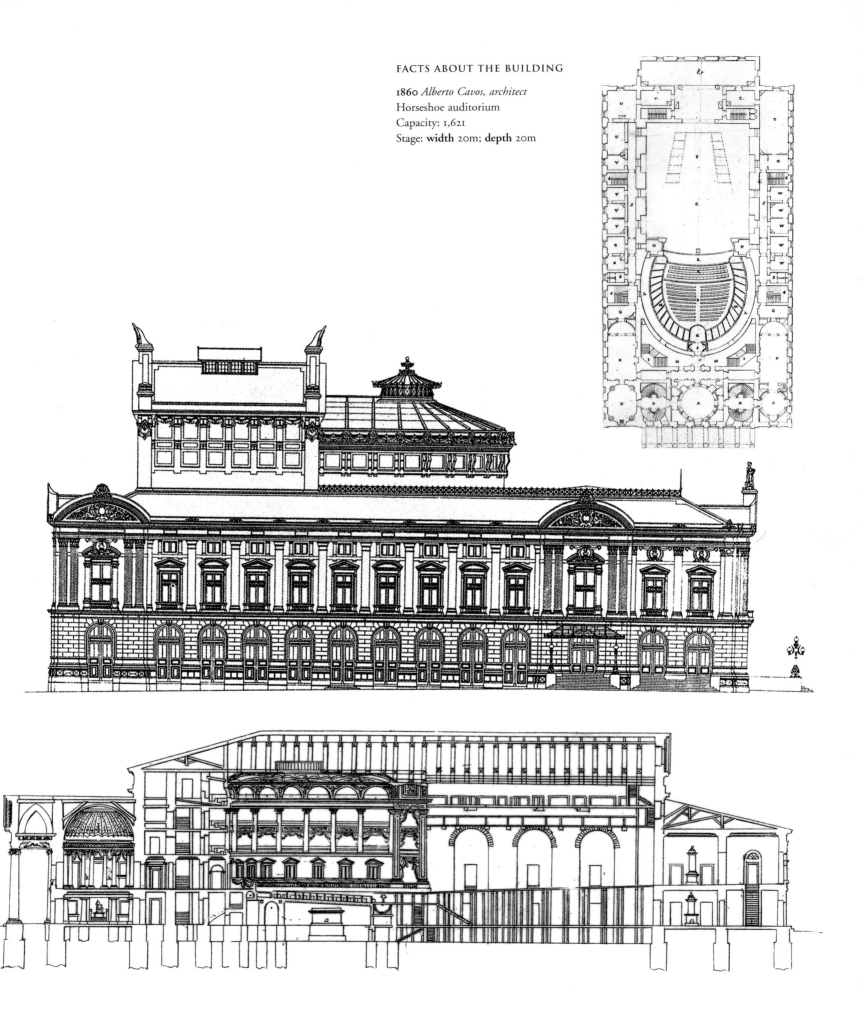

1860 *Alberto Cavos, architect*
Horseshoe auditorium
Capacity: 1,621
Stage: **width** 20m; **depth** 20m

Set design for Moussorgsky's
Khovanshchina by Yuon, in 1913.

Царь-Борисъ-Шаляпинъ, въ послѣднемъ спектаклѣ
въ Парижѣ в маѣ 1913.

From its earliest history in the 18th century, St. Petersburg, a symbol of Russian openness to the West, welcomes operatic troupes from France, Germany, and Italy. During the reign of Catherine the Great, and even later, the new Russian capital pays the highest fees, to both composers and interpreters, in the whole of Europe.

1843. *The Italian Opera Company is formed under the direction of Rubini. Stars on the magnitude of Pauline Viardot, Carlotta Grisi, and Antonio Tamburini often perform in its productions.*

1862. *The world premiere of Verdi's* La Forza del Destino, *a work commissioned for the Maryinsky.*

1871. *On the advice of its Czech music director, Eduard Nápravnik, the Maryinsky rejects Moussorgsky's* Boris Godunov. *This masterpiece would not be performed in St. Petersburg until three years later.*

1911. *The world premiere, on 7 November, of Moussorgsky's* Khovanshchina, *fifteen years after its first private performance in 1886. The composer had begun work on this vast panorama of Russian history in 1872 but had left it unfinished at his death in 1881. In 1882 Rimsky-Korsakov took over the project and orchestrated the score, modifying it along the way. In 1960, Shostakovich prepared a new edition, more faithful to the original.*

1925. *The first "Soviet" operas receive their world premieres, at the same time as classic works are being retitled, such as Puccini's* Tosca, *which becomes* The Struggle for the Commune.

1934. *The world premiere of Shostakovich's* Katerina Ismailova (Lady Macbeth of Mtsensk). *Stalin and Zhdanov, shocked by the lurid subject matter as well as by the strident modernism of the music, ban the production and even close the Kirov.*

1946. *Postwar reopening. Shortly thereafter the Kirov gives the first performance of Prokoviev's opera* Bethrothal in a Monastery, *while the Maly Theatre introduces the composer's* War and Peace.

Dresden and Garnier in Paris, wanted to erect the largest theatre ever seen, a monster venue doomed to remain on paper. The Revolution of 1917 turned St. Petersburg into Petrograd and the Maryinksy into the National Academy of Opera and Ballet, which soon emerged as a showcase for Soviet spectacles. In 1924 Peter the Great's "window on the West" found itself retitled once again, this time Leningrad, but the Maryinsky retained its title for another ten years before it became the Kirov, a house rededicated to the classics as well as to new works officially sanctioned by the regime. Closed during World War II, the Kirov was not rehabilitated until 1963, a process that lasted until 1970. However, it took the collapse of Communism in 1990 for both the city and its leading theatre to recover their original names, which for the Maryinsky brought an end to the most wrenching identity crisis in the history of opera.

III Europe's Model Theatres

Teatro Comunale
Bologna

TEATRO COMUNALE
Bologna - Italy

To replace the Teatro Malvezzi, destroyed by fire in 1745, the Bolognese nobility, with financial guarantees from the local Senate, as well as the Vatican, called on Antonio Galli-Bibiena, heir to a native dynasty of builders and designers whose name had become legendary during the first half of the 18th century. The founder of the family, Ferdinando, together with his brother Francesco, had introduced trompel'oeil scenery to the stage, thereby revolutionizing operatic décor. More importantly, Ferdinando had also devised a new system of graduated boxes and perfected the bell-plan auditorium, which his sons, under Habsburg patronage, spread throughout Europe, where it became known as theatre *à l'italienne*. The Teatro Comunale in Bologna was the first test of Antonio's powers, before he went on to build the opera house in Pavia and the Teatro Scientifico in Mantua, which won the praise of Mozart himself. In 1756 Antonio presented his Bolognese patrons with a scale model for a very audacious project. Alas, his attempts to persuade his patrons proved futile and he had to reduce his plans for the façades. He used stone exclusively, as a defense against fire, the

result of which was a hall with the aspect of a Baroque building turned inside out. The tiered boxes were to have risen above a rusticated arcade, their posts and arches linked together about a proscenium with grandiose portals and statues recalling the Palladian theatre in Vicenza. Finally, however, Galli-Bibiena had to settle for a simplified version, whereby the boxes would not

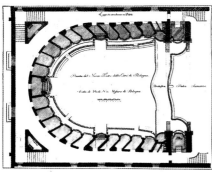

so much rise with the vertical thrust of bays as align horizontally in the way of traditional balconies. Meanwhile, the forestage also had to be reduced, which offered the compensating benefit of a larger proscenium. Inaugurated on 14 May 1763, with Gluck conducting a performance of his *Il Trionfo di Clelia*, the Comunale remained more or less has it had been created until around 1820, when it underwent substantial modification. At the end of the 19th century the house emerged as a champion of Wagner and thus a stronghold of opposition to the almighty Verdi. After fire ravaged the stage in 1931, Bologna saw an opportunity to reclaim the classical purity envisioned by Antonio Galli-Bibiena, a task assumed by Umberto Rizzi, albeit without realizing the entire theatre as originally planned.

FACTS ABOUT THE BUILDING

1763 *Antonio Galli-Bibiena, architect, and M. Galletti, builder*
1820 *G. Tubertini, architect*
1854 *C. Parmigiani, architect*
1935 *Umberto Rizzi, architect*
Capacity: 1,000
Horseshoe auditorium
Proscenium: **width** 15m; **height** 9.50m
Stage: **width** 24m; **height** 29m; **depth** 22m

Bologna gained several new theatres in the course of the 18th century, among them the Marsigli Rossi, the Malvezzi, and the Formagliari. It had long been the custom for Italian conductors and singers to begin the autumn season with performances in Bologna, before proceeding to other opera houses in Italy. This made Bologna a magnet for impresarios in search of new talents, composers as well as conductors. The most famous singer of the period was Maria Maddalena Musi, nicknamed La Mignatto—'the Bloodsucker'!

At the end of the 19th century, great tenors such as Caruso performed on the Bolognese stage, a tradition that would continue in the 20th century with Gigli, Pertile, and Schipa, among others.

1871. Angelo Mariani, following his quarrel with Verdi, introduced Wagner to Italy when he conducted performances of Lohengrin in Bologna, and then Tannhäuser the next year. Thereafter Bologna remained a Wagner stronghold until the end of the century, with The Flying Dutchman given there in 1877, Tristan in 1888, and Parsifal in 1914. Indeed, the city became a bastion of resistance to Verdi, particularly in 1875 when the second version of Boito's Mefistofele proved a triumph, with the composer hailed as the true rival of Verdi.

Nevertheless, Bologna gave Don Carlos its first performance in Italy, on 27 October, only a few months after the premiere in Paris, which had commissioned the opera, one of Verdi's grandest.

In the 1960s, the Teatro Comunale produced rare and forgotten works by Rossini, Bellini, and Donizetti, thanks to the policies of conductors Pietro Rattalino and Riccardo Chailly. Then came the daringly imaginative productions of the stage director Luca Ronconi, who found a home in Bologna at an early date, beginning with Gounod's Faust in 1975.

Set for *Didone abbandonata* by Giuseppe Galli-Bibiena (late 17th-early 18th century).

Teatro alla Scala
Milan

1776. *Milan's ducal theatre burns to the ground on 26 February. The box-holders commission the architect Giuseppe Piermarini to draw up plans for the Teatro alla Scala.*

1778. *Inaugurated on 3 August with Salieri's* L'Europa Riconosciuta.

1807-1814. *L. Canonica enlarges the stage.*

1838. *The stage machinery is modernized.*

1857. *Adjacent structures are removed, allowing La Scala to open on to a newly created plaza.*

1921. *The privilege of owning a box is abolished, thereby doing away with a the system that had long controlled the sale and distribution of tickets. La Scala becomes an* Ente autonomo (*an official agency responsible for managing the theatre*).

1943. *La Scala is damaged by Allied air raids during the nights of 15 and 16 August.*

1946. *When the house reopens on 11 May it boasts a higher as well as a wider stage and an enlarged orchestra pit. Both the foyer and the vestibules have been modified.*

1955. *Architect Piero Portaluppi creates the Piccola Scala, a 600-seat theatre, in the left wing of the big opera house. It opens with Cimarosa's* Il Matrimonio Segreto.

S tendhal, writing in 1817, was the first to predict that La Scala in Milan would become the Mecca of both singers and opera lovers. The capital of Lombardy boasts an operatic history going back to 1717, when its Austrian overlords built the Teatro Regio Ducal, a court theatre in which Mozart and Gluck won their first international fame. In 1776 the Regio burned to the ground one night during Carnival. Pressured by Empress Maria-Theresa, the nobility decided to erect not just one theatre but two of them, the first, La Canobbiano, reserved for the court and the second open to the bourgeoisie. This venue, a much larger affair, was to be located on the site of the former Santa Maria della Scala Church, and it was from this that the new opera house took its name. The same architect, Giuseppe Piermarini, drew up plans for both theatres; for La Scala he merely recast his Neoclassical formula on a monumental scale. The result was to prove a model, a symbol of rediscovered identity, which, by the end of the 18th century, would be imitated everywhere from Lisbon to London. The façade was all but indistinguishable from that of the palace next door; more significantly, it gave no hint of the sumptuous auditorium within, containing three thousand or so seats, upon which the curtain rose on 3 August 1778 for the inaugural performance of Antonio Salieri's *L'Europa Riconosciuta*. A ring of floor-level boxes, four tiers of regular boxes, where no end of ices were consumed during performances, and a top gallery rose about a horseshoe space in which the audience occupying the orchestra or stall

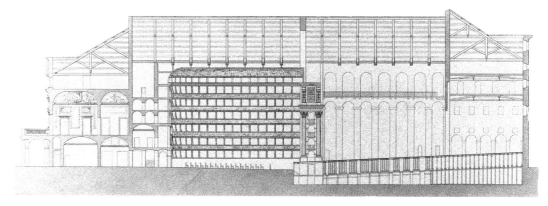

The auditorium of La Scala, Milan, by Durelli.

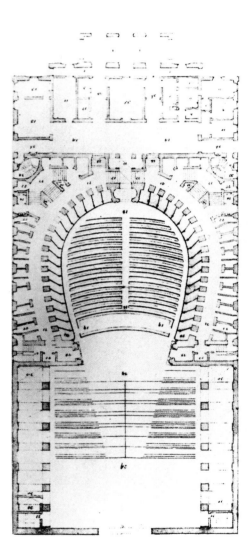

FACTS ABOUT THE BUILDING

1778 *Giuseppe Piermarini, architect*
1955 *Piero Portaluppi, architect of La Piccola Scala*
Capacity: 2,800
Horseshoe auditorium
Six tiers of boxes
Proscenium: **width** 16m; **height** 10m
Stage: **width** 26m; **height** 27m; **depth** 20m

Maria Callas in *Tosca.*

benches enjoyed ideal acoustics. At the center of the horseshoe was, of course, the "royal" box, which glittered or remained curtained according to Austria's success on the battlefield. As the years rolled by, La Scala had its backstage enlarged in 1807, its interior redecorated by Sanquirico in 1830, and its stage machinery updated in 1838. The great house was also freed in 1857 from the buildings that hemmed it in and liberated, in 1921, from the privileged few who had long held their boxes as personal property. La Scala also played an important role in the drama of Italian unification, the Risorgimento, that initiated the tradition whereby La Scala begins every season on 7 December, the feast day of Saint Ambrose, the patron saint of Milan. Piermarini's theatre survived without major physical damage until 1943, when it took

a direct hit from Allied bombers, but restoration was underway even before the war was over. The fly-tower was heightened, though this spoiled the purity of the roofline outside. The orchestra pit was also enlarged and the foyers redesigned. In 1946 La Scala reopened under the baton of Arturo Toscanini. It was to him that the Piccola Scala would be dedicated ten years later, a little 600-seat theatre carved out of La Scala's left wing by the architect Piero Portaluppi. The opening performance of every season is universally regarded as the major event of Italian operatic life.

auditorium. Thanks to its productions, and to the encounters and affairs that took place there, La Scala enjoyed the loyal patronage of high bourgeoisie and nobility alike. Early in the 19th century La Scala established its reputation with premieres of major works by Rossini, Donizetti, Meyerbeer, and Mercadante. **1824-1826.** *The regime of English impresario Joseph Glossop, during which La Scala stages some 250 performances of operas by Gioachino Rossini.*

1826-1832. *The regime of Domenico Barbaia commissions works from Vincenzo Bellini, among them* Il Pirata *and* Norma.

1836-1850, 1861-1863. *The regime of Bartolomeo Merelli, which commissions* Oberto *and* Nabucco *as well as two other operas from Giuseppe Verdi. Premiered on 9 March 1842,* Nabucco *establishes a record that remains unbroken in the annals of La Scala: a run of 65 performances. The famous chorus "Va, pensiero" becomes the unofficial national anthem of Risorgimento Italy.*

1898-1903, 1906-1908, 1920-1929. *Under the conductor Arturo Toscanini, La Scala enjoys three separate periods of great critical and popular success. Toscanini added Wagner to the repertory and staged the Italian premieres of Tchaikovsky's* Eugene Onegin, *Strauss's* Salome, *and Debussy's* Pelléas et Mélisande. *He also conducted the world premieres of operas by Pizzetti, Boito, Respighi, Giordano, and Zandonai. The most memorable premiere of all may have been that of Puccini's* Turandot *(1926), when the maestro stopped the performance at the point in the third act where the deceased composer left his score unfinished, despite an ending prepared by Franco Alfano at Toscanini's request.*

1930-1957. *Victor De Sabata succeeded Toscanini as music director.*

1946. *La Scala reopens with Verdi's* Requiem, *conducted by Toscanini. Renata Tabaldi makes her Scala debut in the soprano part.*

1946-1972. *The regime of Antonio Ghirengelli, during which Maria Callas (1950-1958) stars in a series of celebrated productions, among them: Spontini's* La Vestale, *Donizetti's* Anna Bolena, *Bellini's* La Sonnambula, *and Verdi's* La Traviata, *all directed by Luchino Visconti, with Carlo Maria Giulini on the podium for* Sonnambula *and* Traviata.

1971-1980. *Claudio Abbado, music director.*

1986—. *Riccardo Muti, music director.*

Luciano Pavarotti and Gabriel Bacquier in Donizetti's *L'Elisir d'Amore.*

Staatsoper Dresden

1841. *The theatre designed by Gottfried Semper is inaugurated for the first time.*
1869. *Dresden's opera house burns to the ground.*
1878. *The reconstructed theatre is inaugurated. Semper preserves the overall form of the original building.*
1918. *Semper's theatre becomes the Dresden Staatsoper.*
1945. *Allied bombing demolishes the building. The opera company moves to the city hall and performs there until 1948, when it moves to the reconstructed Schauspielhaus.*
1985. *Again rebuilt from Semper's plans, the opera house is inaugurated a third time.*

Gottfried Semper was one of the few architects who lived to see his opera house built twice within only 35 years. There had been about ten previous theatres in the vicinity of the royal palace in Dresden. Semper built his own first theatre in 1841. A year later Wagner staged the premiere of his opera *Rienzi* and was soon appointed Kapellmeister to the Grand Duke of Saxony. The idyllic period that followed lasted several years, until Wagner had to flee because of his role in the revolution of 1848. After Semper joined Wagner in Zurich, the two artists set about refining their ideas for a theatre of the future. The future, as it turned out, would divide the collaborators once their immense project for Munich fell through. While Wagner took the path that eventually led him to Bayreuth, Semper returned to Dresden, where his theatre had burned in 1869. Planning anew, he rebuilt the house and saw it reopen in 1878. Like the earlier structure, it stood opposite the court chapel to which its façade, rounded like the apse of a church, made a kind of antiphonal response. Beyond the two arcaded stories and the set-back attic lay staircases placed like transepts on either side of the auditorium, under a roof as imposing as that over a cathedral nave. Thirty years later Semper preserved the general form of his first theatre, even though he added an entrance porch and a crowning quadriga to a still convex but lighter façade and heightened the stage until it thrust like a bell tower above the once-unified roofline. Despite the external appearances, the auditorium did not exactly follow the curve of the façade. Semper, it seems, either could not or did not wish to adopt the ideas of Wagner; instead, he remained loyal to the Italian style of theatre design. Nevertheless, the lessons of Bayreuth were not entirely lost at Dresden; the top gallery was treated like a gigantic amphitheatre or a second stalls section, thereby making the house more democratically inclusive. Still, history had not finished with Dresden. In 1945 aerial bombardment reduced the theatre to rubble. Once again, Semper came to the rescue from beyond the grave. Paradoxically it was a Communist regime in decline that oversaw the scrupulous re-creation of a building deeply symbolic of bourgeois ideals. The

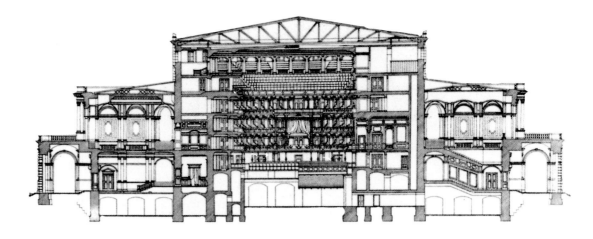

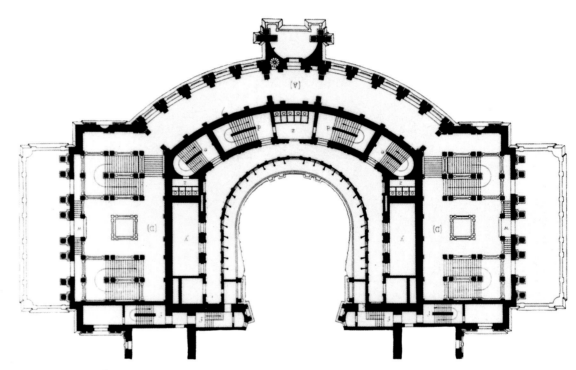

1842. *On 20 October, thirty-year-old Richard Wagner conducts the premiere of* Rienzi, *an opera based on the Bulwer Lytton novel. So promising was the work that the Dresden Court Opera offered to produce it as soon as it had been completed. Heading the cast were Joseph Tichatschek, tenor, and Wilhelmine Schröder-Devrient, a soprano who had made a strong impression on Wagner fourteen years earlier when he heard her sing Bellini. Much taken with her voice, the budding composer sent Schröder-Devrient a letter in which he declared that she had given direction to his artistic life and should always remember that she alone had inspired his vocation.* Rienzi *triumphed despite lasting six hours. If the characters seem now to anticipate the Wagnerian heroes of later operas, the composer would soon vigorously disown them, questioning how he could possibly have created "an opera so full of bombast." Thus he wrote to his friend Franz Liszt: "Neither as an artist nor as a man do I have the heart to revise this work, which now strikes me as so outmoded, and which I have already had to refashion more than once because of its immoderate dimensions. I no longer have the courage, and hope with all my soul to replace it with something new." Wagner spoke of* Rienzi *as if it were almost a youthful aberration.*

1843. *After the premiere of* The Flying Dutchman, *Wagner becomes music director of the Dresden Court Opera. He is also named Kappellmeister to the Grand Duke of Saxony, a title once held by Carl Maria von Weber.*

1845. *Wagner's* Tannhäuser *receives its premiere, with Schröder-Devrient and Tichatschek again in the cast, but the opera fails. The composer believes himself to be the victim of a conspiracy; meanwhile, his official position causes irritation, and his political ideas give offense. The situation grows worse when he decides to conduct Beethoven's Ninth Symphony, long regarded as unplayable. Yet, the concert proves a great success, confirming Wagner's talent as a conductor. This allows him to remount* Tannhäuser, *which is now greeted with favor.*

restoration, which included statuary, mosaics and painting, is regarded as a model of what modern craftsmanship can achieve. The various rehearsal halls and workshops have been relegated to buildings in the neighborhood, which clears the stage itself of all unnecessary clutter.

FACTS ABOUT THE BUILDING

1841 *Gottfried Semper, architect*
1878 *Gottfried Semper, architect*
1985 *Reconstruction from Semper's original plans*
Capacity: 1,309
Horseshoe auditorium
Stage: **width** 16m; **height** 16m; **depth** 22m

1901-1945. *Richard Strauss directs the Dresden Opera, where he is also the house composer, there creating the great majority of his works.*

Premieres of operas by Richard Strauss:

1905. Salome.

1909. Elektra, *an opera based on Sophocles but with a libretto by Hugo von Hofmannsthal. Ernestine Schumann-Heink, who created the role of Klytemnestra, later declared: "I shall never again sing that role. It was horrible. We were a band of madwomen. . . . Nothing can go any further than* Elektra. *Wagner had taken us to the extreme limit of dramatic writing for the voice. But Strauss has gone beyond that. His voices are lost. We are blocked. I think Strauss himself realizes this." History records, however, that during the dress rehearsal, Strauss shouted at the orchestra: "Louder! I can still hear Madame Heink!"*

1911. Der Rosenkavalier.

1924. Intermezzo *with Lotte Lehmann.*

1928. Die Aegyptische Helene (The Egyptian Helen).

1933. Arabella.

1935. Die Schweigsame Frau (The Silent Woman).

1938. Daphne.

1944. *At the end of the summer, during preparations for the premiere of* Die Liebe der Danae (the Love of Danae), *the Nazis order the closure of all theatres. On 16 August Clemens Krauss conducts the entire opera in rehearsal, but the formal premiere would not come until eight years later at the Salzburg Festival.*

1985. *Semper's rebuilt opera house reopens in February with a performance of Carl Maria von Weber's* Der Freischütz, *the last work performed before the destruction of the Dresden Staatsoper.*

Elisabeth Schwarzkopf after a performance of Strauss's *Der Rosenkavelier.*

Eva Marton in Strauss's *Elektra* in 1992.

Staatsoper Vienna

STAATSOPER
Vienna - Austria

1857. The great project of urban renewal is launched within the city center. It would include the construction of a new opera house near the Käntnertortheater.

1860. Emperor Franz Joseph opens a competition for the design of an opera house along the Ringstrasse recently built on the foundations of the old encircling city ramparts. The winners of the competition are Eduard van der Nüll and August Siccard von Siccardsburg. Moritz von Schwind would execute the murals around the grand stairway and the loggia, leaving C. Rahl to paint the ceiling.

1869. Inaugurated on 25 May with Mozart's Don Giovanni *sung in German.*

1945. Fire breaks out following an aerial bombardment by the Allies. The façades, the foyer, the former court ballroom, the loggia frescoes, and the grand stairway survive. Erich Beltenstern is commissioned to rebuild and enlarge the Staatsoper. The marble hall would be decorated by Otto Prossinger, the Gobelins room by Zeno Kossak, and the drop curtain painted by Rudolf Eisenmanger.

1955. The rebuilt theatre is inaugurated on 5 November with Beethoven's Fidelio.

Vienna in the second half of the 19th century was not merely the Waltz Queen of Europe; she was also the Queen of Opera. When, in 1857, Emperor Franz Joseph ordered the demolition of Vienna's ancient circle of defensive walls, which had long strangled the heart of the city, and their replacement by a wide boulevard, the Ringstrasse, the first official building completed there would be the Hofoper, or Court Opera, not Parliament or City Hall. Here the new church, university, and public buildings could be viewed as a triumph for Habsburg prestige and the power of Austrian liberalism. With their stylistic eclecticism, heavily dosed with the Italian Renaissance, they constituted a kind of *Bildungsideal* in which both the aristocracy and the rising bourgeoisie could see themselves represented. The archetypal symbol of this development was the opera house, built by Eduard van der Nüll and August Siccard von Siccardsburg, who openly declared their

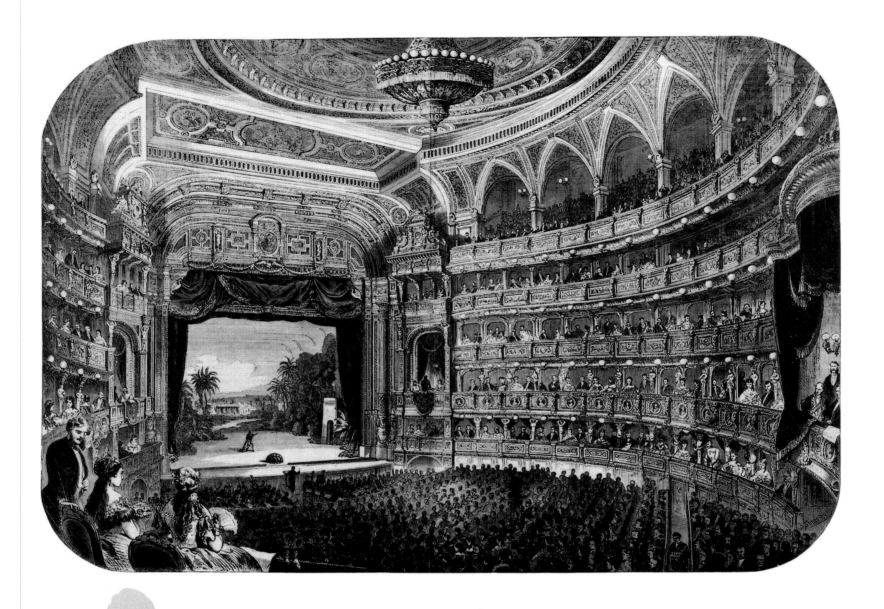

The auditorium of the Vienna Opera House, by M.B. Strassberger.

1870. *The Viennese premiere of Wagner's* Die Meistersinger von Nürnberg, *under the direction of Johan von Herbeck (director of the Vienna Court Opera). The preparation takes five weeks and nineteen orchestra rehearsals.*

1872. *Richard Wagner conducts a program of excerpts from his own operas. The event becomes the stuff of legend because of the cracking big storm that broke out during the famous 'Ride of the Valkyries,' prompting the composer to view the commotion in the sky as a favorable sign for his Bayreuth plans! He had already paid tribute to the Philharmonic at the Viennese premiere of* Lohengrin. *In his 1869 essay on*

reliance on Vicenza's Palladian Basilica for their façade. Neither architect, however, was present when the new theatre opened, on 25 May 1869, with a performance of Mozart's *Don Giovanni* sung in German: the first had committed suicide, and the second, it was said, died of mortification over the negative reaction to his masterpiece. Not even the Emperor spared the architects, declaring that the great house looked as if it were sinking. The interior, on the other hand, won universal praise. Indeed, nothing could be said against the beauty of the grand stairway, the luxurious salons, or the quality of the traditional, Italian-style auditorium with its four tiers of boxes. Renamed the Staatsoper in 1918, Vienna's opera house could survive the collapse of the Austrian Empire but not the aerial bombardments of World War II. This set off a lively debate over what kind of reconstruction should follow. The modernists, led by Josef Hoffmann, wanted to sweep away the past, whereas the Salzburg architect Clemens Holzmeister proposed erecting an auditorium with a deep, gallery-like balcony. Finally, Austria sided with the conservatives, who advocated a neutral solution. Thus, when the company returned to their own stage in November 1955, after five years at the Theater an der Wien, they found themselves performing Beethoven's *Fidelio* in a theatre whose staircase,

conducting, the composer had also declared the orchestra to be 'the greatest in the world.'

1892. *Premiere of Massenet's* Werther, *sung in German.*

1897. *Gustav Mahler is appointed director of the Hofoper, the Vienna Court Opera.*

1918. *The Hofoper becomes the Staatsoper.*

1929-1942. *Clemens Krauss, Felix Weingartner, and Bruno Walter succeed one another as principal conductor of the Vienna Philharmonic.*

1943. *Karl Böhm is named director of the Staatsoper.*

1944. *Hans Knappertsbusch conducts Wagner's* Götterdämmerung, *after which the authorities close the theatre.*

1954. *Karl Böhm resumes his role as director, only to abandon it two years later.*

1955. *The rebuilt opera house is inaugurated with Beethoven's* Fidelio, *directed by Heinz Tietjen and conducted by Karl Böhm. The performance becomes a major event in the history of postwar Europe, in large part because* Fidelio, *with its chorus of prisoners, could serve as the symbol of a country from which the occupying armies had just departed. The inaugural festival, dubbed a Musical Coronation, becomes an international media event.*

1956. *Herbert von Karajan becomes director of the Staatsoper, decreeing that operas should be sung in their original languages. He also initiates the sta-gione system, using specially assembled casts for each new production, instead of casting all roles from the house roster.*

1981. *Karl Böhm decides at the end of his career to conduct Richard Strauss's* Elektra, *with Leonie Rysanek in the title role, and make it a sort of final testament to Vienna. The production would be immortalized in a video filmed by Götz Friedrich. During rehearsals Böhm said to the soprano: 'You have the voice that Strauss dreamed of hearing in his music. If he had heard you, he would have composed an opera for you.'*

The auditorium of the Vienna Opera House during a performance of Wagner's *Mastersingers*. Watercolour by Oskar Laske, 1930s.

foyer and public rooms appeared to be the same Staatsoper of old, but the auditorium dramatically simplified. Continuity does not, after all, mean resistance to progress, and so the theatre boasts, hidden away under its huge stage and backstage, a vast array of the most up-to-date, computer-driven hydraulic machinery, a system later adopted for La Scala in Milan. Still, if Vienna remains unrivaled as a temple of operatic art, it is owing less to the *Bogenstil* atmosphere of the house than to its prestigious casts, as well as to all the great conductors who, from Mahler through Weingartner, Strauss, Böhm, and Karajan to Bernstein, Maazel, and Abbado, have succeeded one another on the podium of the legendary Vienna Philharmonic, a permanent and indispensable presence in the orchestra pit.

Richard Wagner at the first night of *The Mastersingers*.

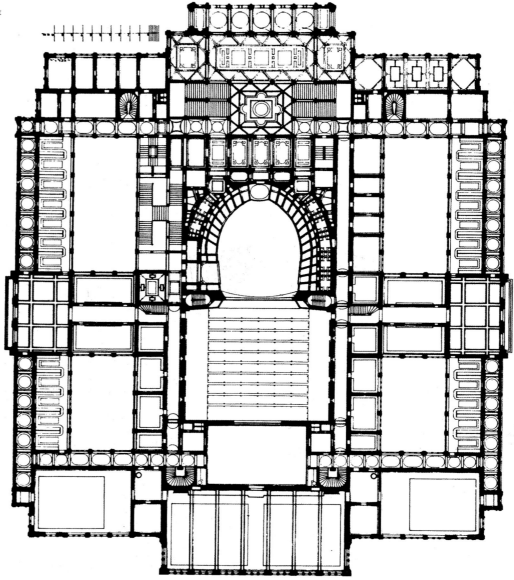

FACTS ABOUT THE BUILDING

1869 *Eduard van der Nüll and August Siccard von Siccardsburg*
1955 *Erich Boltenstern*
Capacity: *2,276*
Horseshoe auditorium
Proscenium: **width** *13*m; **height** *12*m
Stage: **width** *27.50*m; **depth** *22.50*m; **height** *22.50*m

Kiri Te Kanawa and Jane Barbier in *Così fan tutte*, production by Giorgio Strehler.

Palais Garnier Opéra National de Paris

1858. *The large Opéra de Paris is authorized.*

1861. *Charles Garnier wins the design competition on 29 May.*

1862. *Construction begins on a site measuring 12,000 square metres. The total cost would come to 49 million francs, including payments to the 13 painters and 89 sculptors engaged to decorate the grand staircase.*

1875. *Inaugurated on 5 January with a program that includes one act of Halévy's* La Juive *and excerpts from Meyerbeer's* Les Huguenots.

1962. *André Malraux commissions Marc Chagall to execute a new painting for the dome over the auditorium. The work is done in 1964 on a plastic shell designed to leave a 10cm space between it and Jules-Eugène Lenepveu's original painting, which is thereby carefully preserved.*

1969. *The electrical systems are completely overhauled.*

1988. *Architect Jean-Loup Roubert creates two floors of dance studios in the once empty space under the great dome. An electronic organ and telecast facilities are also introduced.*

1995. *The stage's technical equipment is updated, and the paintings, gilding, seats, and boxes are all restored.*

Since 1669, when Louis XIV authorized the Abbé Pierre Perrin to form the Opéra de Paris, the company has performed on some fifteen different stages, but the theatre built by Charles Garnier in the 1860s was the first to bear the title "Palais." Napoleon III liked to think big, especially in 1858 when he was still smarting from a recent attempt on his life, made just outside the Salle Le Peletier, the old opera (which later burnt down in 1873). The Emperor ordered Baron Haussmann to clear a site for the future opera house, at the very center of the elegant new quarters then being built on the western edge of the capital. Opened to competition, the project proved a magnet for the very best of

contemporary architects, among them Viollet-le-Duc, an established master favored by the Empress Eugénie. Yet, it was an unknown candidate, Charles Garnier, just back from postgraduate studies in Rome and Athens, who won the commission with his clever combination of functional planning and Second Empire taste. Construction went on for fifteen years, delayed at first by underground water, which took weeks to pump before the foundations could be laid. Then came the Commune (1871), which turned Garnier's Opéra into a warehouse and prison during the siege of Paris. As a result it was the

FACTS ABOUT THE BUILDING

1875 *Charles Garnier, architect*
1959 *Bailleau, architect of the first rehearsal studio built under the great dome*
1988 and **1995** *Jean-Loup Roubert, architect*

Horseshoe auditorium
Capacity: 1,979
1 balcony and 5 tiers of boxes
Proscenium: **width** 13.25m; **height** 9.80cm
Stage: **width** 32m; **height** 34m; **depth** 24.50m

Third Republic, under President Mac-Mahon, which in 1875 would finally inaugurate what the defunct Empire had begun. On the exterior, the structure is clearly legible, rising from the entrance arcade through the colonnade enclosing the grand foyer and the dome over the auditorium to the top of the stage building, the entire mass flanked by two rotundas, one designed for the Emperor's private use and the other as an entrance for subscribers. Inside, the Palais Garnier embodies a crimson and gold dream, the dream of that bourgeoisie whom Offenbach so gleefully lampooned on other stages in Paris. When the Empress questioned Garnier about the interior—"What is this? It's not a style!"—the architect replied: "It's Napoleon III." To create it, he had recruited his onetime fellow *pensionnaires* at the French Academy in Rome—

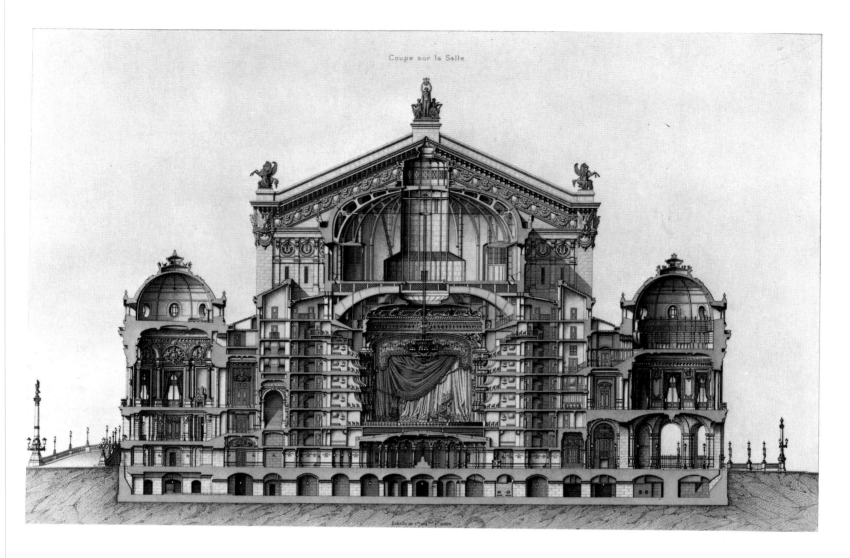

Coupe sur la Salle

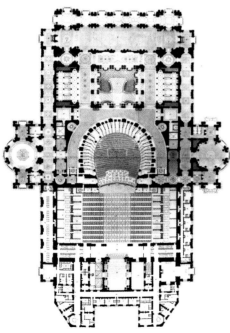

Pils, Baudry, Lenepveu, Delaunay, and other exponents of official art—and set them to work decorating the galleries and salons. More importantly, Garnier consulted the achievements of Victor Louis, particularly in Bordeaux, when he designed the building's overall silhouette, the magnificence of the grand staircase, and in the innovative use of iron to reinforce stone masonry. But when it came to the auditorium's acoustics and the metal scaffolding for stage machinery, he relied solely on his own intuition and his travels throughout Europe. Funds were not available to place the stage on jacks, those precursors of the present elevator system. And he gave up the idea of covering the orchestra as Wagner was doing at the Festspielhaus in Bayreuth, a theatre Garnier took as a partial model when he designed the Opéra de Monte Carlo. Miraculously untouched by time, the "Nouvel Opéra" has come down to us precisely as the architect left it, save for the painting on the ceiling over the auditorium, where the original gave way in 1964 to a work by Chagall. The huge dome now houses dance studios, whereas it had been an empty space used only for cleaning the famous chandelier. An Emperor's dream and the joy of the bourgeoisie, all that it lacked was appeal to the common people, an appeal that has now been supplied by the new opera house at the Bastille.

Teresa Stratas in Berg's *Lulu*, produced by Patrice Chéreau at the Palais Garnier, Paris, in 1979.

1875. President Mac-Mahon awards Charles Garnier the Cross of the Legion of Honor on the evening the new Opéra is inaugurated. Originally called the Salle des Capucines, because of its location on the Boulevard des Capucines, the great house would later be known as the "Palais" Garnier, in acknowledgment of its extraordinary opulence.

1881. The auditorium is lit by electricity, as would be the stage in 1887. A performance is telephonically transmitted for the first time.

1915. Jacques Rouché begins his thirty-year tenure as director of the Opéra. He would be the last to manage the theatre as a concession.

1918. Marthe Chenal sings La Marseillaise *on the front steps to celebrate the Armistice.*

1958. Maria Callas makes her debut at the Opéra, the last of the great stages on which she would reign supreme, singing the first act of Norma, *the second act of* La Tosca, *and the third act of* Il Trovatore.

1965. Callas gives her final performance in Paris as Tosca. It is an extra performance added to satisfy the huge public demand for a chance to see la diva des divas.

1973. Rolf Liebermann takes charge of the Opéra and remains there until 1980. He reinstates a policy of engaging only the very best singers and of performing operas exclusively in their original languages. He also insists upon recruiting the greatest conductors, as well as the most outrageous set and costume designers.

1973. Giorgio Strehler's celebrated production of The Marriage of Figaro *receives its first performance, conducted by Georg Solti.*

1979. The complete version of Alban Berg's Lulu *is performed for the first time anywhere, in a production designed by Patrice Chéreau. Teresa Stratas sings the title role under the baton of Pierre Boulez.*

1983. The world premiere of Olivier Messiaen's Saint François d'Assise, *conducted by Seiji Ozawa.*

1989. Henceforth the Opéra National de Paris gives performances at the new Opéra Bastille while the Palais Garnier specializes in ballet.

IV Inheriting a Tradition

Deutsche Staatsoper Berlin

1741. *Georg Wenzeslaus von Knobelsdorff builds the Berlin Hofoper, or Court Opera, for King Frederick II of Prussia.*

1742. *Inaugurated on 7 December with Carl Heinrich Graun's* Cleopatra e Cesare.

1788. *Carl Gotthard Langhans enlarges the galleries.*

1843. *Fire destroys the Berlin Court Opera.*

1844. *Carl Ferdinand Langhans reconstructs the fire-ravaged opera house, extending the building on either side to allow for the introduction of staircases. He also raises the roof in order to add a fourth balcony and eliminates the ground-floor boxes. The Court Opera reopens with Giacomo Meyerbeer's* Ein Feldlager in Schlesien.

1910. *The stage building is heightened.*

1928. *Eduard Fürstenau erects the side and back stages, a campaign of building and improvement that places the Berlin Staatsoper at the forefront of German scenography.*

1935. *Paul Baumgarten is commissioned to renovate the vestibule and foyer in the Nazi taste.*

1941. *Damaged by aerial bombardment in April. Schwiezer, Salexki, and Seydel oversee the restoration, which includes a conversion of the vestibule into a foyer for the downstairs section of the auditorium.*

Today Berlin lives peacefully with three rival opera houses, but peace had little to do with one of those theatres—the Staatsoper—whose history unfolded to the sound of thundering cannons. The War of the Austrian Succession had been under way for two years when, in December 1742, Frederick II, soon to be Frederick the Great, received the keys to the new Hofoper designed by his friend Baron von Knobelsdorff. With its Corinthian portico and relief-carved pediment, Berlin's Court Opera survives as one of the earliest manifestations of Germany's nascent classicism, standing on the future Unter den Linden, as if it were to be a vantage point for reviewing troops. As the inaugural opera, Graun's *Cleopatra e Cesare*, announced, the house would be dedicated to Italian opera; it would be available only to the aristocracy, who had exclusive use of the single foyer, the Apollosaal, and to military officers. The auditorium, however, despite a plan based upon a prototype by Antonio Galli-Bibiena, was a disappointment, its precious space invaded by an aggressively projected forestage. In 1788 Carl Langhans the Elder refashioned it, installing seats in the orchestra stalls, transforming the galleries into deep balconies, partitioning the boxes in the French manner, and paring back the forestage to create a royal box. After a fire in 1843 the task of reconstruction fell to Carl Langhans the Younger, with orders from Frederick William IV not to touch the façades or to raise the roofs, although brief lateral wings could be added to house staircases. The auditorium lost its downstairs boxes but gained a fourth balcony on top, while the forestage had once again to give way, this time to allow for new contiguous boxes. A half-century later, at the dawn of another war, the lack of backstage space became so intolerable that the sober temple of old suffered the indignity of having a square, windowless stage tower added at the back. At the end of the 1920s Eduard Fürstenau extended the theatre, now the Staatsoper, along the sides, again to enlarge the stage, both laterally and in depth. In 1935 the Third Reich had the public areas redecorated in its own Nazi style, all of which would disappear in 1941 when a bomb fell on the Staatsoper, reducing it to a heap of rubble. Thus, two centuries after its inauguration, the reconstruction of Berlin's main opera house again became a wartime project, although, for the want of funds,

1942. *The restored Staatsoper inaugurated with Wagner's* Die Meistersinger von Nürnberg.

1945. *In February the Staatsoper is struck anew by Allied bombs.*

1955. *The rebuilt Staatsoper reopens, once more with a performance of* Die Meistersinger. *Again, the renovation is based on the original plans drawn up by Knobelsdorff in the 18th century. Later extensions are preserved. An attic balustrade helps integrate the stage building into the whole. Design improvements are made as well, both in the auditorium and on the stage.*

Three periods of the Berlin Opera House.
Top: general view by Fünck, 18th century.
Centre: project of 1843.
Bottom: enlargement of 1927.

FACTS ABOUT THE BUILDING

1743 *Georg Wenzeslaus von Knobelsdorff, architect*
1788 *Carl Gotthard Langhans, architect*
1844 *Carl Ferdinand Langhans, architect*
1928 *Eduard Fürstenau, architect*
1935 *Paul Baumgarten, architect*
1942 *Schweizer, Salexki, and Seydel, architects*
1955 *Reconstruction completed*

Horseshoe auditorium
Capacity: 1,396
Orchestra stalls and three balconies
Proscenium: **width** 12m; **height** 7.60m
Stage: **width** 23m; **height** 23.45m; **depth** 18m

1871-1934. *During this period Berlin flourishes as a center of German music life, the place where Felix Mendelssohn reintroduces the work of Johann Sebastian Bach to the world audience. Theatres spring up on all sides, their podiums occupied by a succession of great conductor/composers: Carl Maria von Weber, Gaspare Spontini, Giacomo Meyerbeer, and Albert Lortzing. In the 20th century come Felix Weingartner, Carl Muck, Richard Strauss, Leo Blech, and Erich Kleiber, among others.*

1882. *Some fifty rebel musicians come together and create the Berlin Philharmonic, an orchestra governed by the democratic principle of co-responsibility for all members. The musicians elect their conductor and vote on every player eligible for membership. The first conductor elected to lead the orchestra would be Hans von Bülow, beginning in 1887. Among his successors: Johannes Brahms, Edvard Grieg, Gustav Mahler, and Richard Strauss.*

1919. *The Court Opera is renamed the Staatsoper. Contemporary music returns to the repertory.*

1922. *Wilhelm Furtwängler becomes principal conductor of the Berlin Philharmonic and then director of the Staatsoper. Under his regime at the latter would come the world premieres of Alban Berg's* Wozzeck, *on 14 December 1925, and Darius Milhaud's* Christophe Colomb, *on 5 May 1930.*

1955. *Herbert von Karajan is elected permanent conductor and artistic director of the Berlin Philharmonic. The orchestra now enters a Golden Age, its fame and influence confirmed through world tours and classic recordings.*

1989. *Von Karajan dies in October. Claudio Abbado becomes director of the Berlin Philharmonic.*

Herbert von Karajan conducts the Berlin Philharmonic Orchestra.

the colossal theatre proposed by Albert Speer, Hitler's official architect, had to be abandoned in favor of a restoration based on Knobelsdorff's original plans as later modified by Langhans the Younger. In 1945 the war struck again, leaving the theatre so damaged it could not be reopened for another decade, but still in the form it had before, plus extensions that now included a stage building which, with its window openings, flat roof, and attic balustrade, is well integrated with the whole. Meanwhile, the stage equipment represents German scenography at its most advanced.

Teatro *Nacional São Carlos* Lisbon

TEATRO NACIONAL SÃO CARLOS

Lisbon - Portugal

1755. *Lisbon is shaken by a massive earthquake, which destroys the Teatro dos Paços only weeks after its inauguration. The Marquis de Pombal draws up his comprehensive plans for reconstruction.*

1792. *Several rich merchants—the tobacco monopolists Cruz-Sobral, Bandeira Porto-Covo, Pereira Caldas, Machado, and Ferreira-Sola—join with Quintela, the powerful diamond trader from Angola, and commission the architect José Da Costa e Silva to*

ollowing the historic earthquake of 1755, which reduced Lisbon to rubble, the Marquis de Pombal, King Joseph's despotic though enlightened minister, drew up a superbly rational plan of reconstruction consistent with the Neoclassical taste of a bourgeoisie grown rich on overseas trade. Eager to signal its ascendancy, this class took the initiative in 1792 and, through a group of businessmen, raised the funds necessary to build an opera house, where the donors would be allowed the privilege of boxes in perpetuity. Thanks to support from the chief of the royal police, who counted on using profits from the opera for charitable purposes, construction required a mere seven months to complete. The São Carlos opened on 30 June 1793 with a performance of Cimarosa's *La Ballerina Amante*. The theatre would favor the Italian repertory, a preference equally expressed in the overall design and decoration of the house. The name alone discloses that the Portuguese patrons were taking as their model first Naples and then La Scala, where the architect, José Da Costa e Silva, looked carefully at the façade and then virtually copied it for Lisbon. On the bronze-toned interior, the décor reflects the haste with which the building was constructed. However, if Rococo exuberance is lacking, there is a gain in the beautiful unity of the elliptical auditorium dominated by an imposing royal box. With its hemicycle of columns and its dome, this grandiose enclosure suggests a chapel. The São Carlos survived the industrial era largely unscathed by its revolutions, but then fell asleep at the beginning of the 20th century, remaining in its coma until 1946, when the state took control. For all these reasons, the house remains almost as it was the day it first opened, even on the stage, where the old wooden machinery still

Ruins of the opera house after the earthquake and fire of 1755.

design the São Carlos Opera. Construction takes only seven months, thanks to firm support from the influential chief of police, Riogo Inacio Pina de Manique. The ceiling over the atrium (16.30 x 8.70m) is decorated by Cyrillo V. Machado. Above it, the foyer opens on to a terrace. The royal box, in the center, is the work of the Italian G.M. Apiani. Manuel Da Costa designed and executed the ceiling over the auditorium. The stage has no backstage area behind the scenery.

1793. Inaugurated on 30 June with Domenico Cimarosa's La Ballerina Amante.

1940. The theatre reopens following a long period of decline.

1946. The state assumes responsibility for the São Carlos Opera, which now becomes the Teatro Nacional São Carlos.

1958. In March Maria Callas sings Violetta in Verdi's La Traviata, a performance that is recorded and later made famous by Terrance McNalley's play The Lisbon Traviata.

Beginning in the 18th century, opera played an important role in the cultural life of Lisbon, mainly at the very pretty Teatro dos Paços, which opened in 1755, the year of the earthquake, with a performance of David Perez's Alessandro nell'Indie, in a production designed by Giovanni Carlo Bibiena. Portugal, prior to the arrival of native composers of opera, had enjoyed a popular tradition, dating back to the Middle Ages, of plays set to music, a genre known as Vilhancico. Among Portugal's operatic composers must be counted F.A. Almeida (1702-1755), known for La Pazienza di Socrate (1733), La Finta Pazza (1735), and La Spinalba (1739), and A.J. da Silva, who composed La Vida de Don Quichote de la Mancha in 1733, which makes it the first opera with a text in Portuguese.

remains. This harks back to that Age of Enlightenment when, thanks to the determination of a few men, Lisbon saw the castrati light up the Tagus with the fireworks of their pyrotechnical singing.

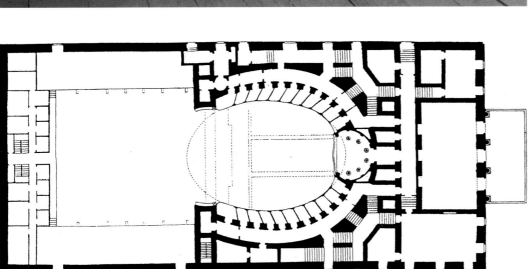

1793. *The São Carlos Opera opens, under the direction of Antonio Leal Moreira. A pupil of Carvalho, Moreira also composed operas, among them* Ascanio in Alba, *which appeared fifteen years after Mozart's opera of the same name.*

1799. *Marco António Portogallo (1762-1830), Moreira's brother-in-law, takes charge of the São Carlos Opera. A composer with an international reputation, Portogallo would write some twenty Italian operas for Lisbon, beginning in 1801.*

The operatic history of the São Carlos resembles that of all the great theatres operating under the influence of Italy.

1970. *Joao de Freitas becomes director of the São Carlos Opera. Since 1970, the Gulbenkian Foundation has fostered the operatic life of Lisbon, and encouraged contemporary composers (Britten, Halfiter, Messaien, Milhaud) through an annual festival.*

FACTS ABOUT THE BUILDING

1793 *José Da Costa e Silva, architect*
Elliptical auditorium
4 tiers of boxes, 1 top balcony, and a royal box
Capacity: 1,100
Proscenium: **width** 13.98m
Stage: **depth** 23.90m

Bayerische Staatsoper
Munich

1811. Maximilian I, King of Bavaria, commissions the architect Karl von Fischer to design a large theatre for the capital city.

1818. Inaugurated on 12 October with Ferdinand Fränzl's Die Weihe.

1823. Fire destroys the theatre on 14 January. The task of reconstruction falls to the Neoclassicist Leo von Klenze, who introduces a second polychrome pediment above and behind the one crowning the portico.

1825. Klenze's reconstructed theatre opens.

1943. Munich and its opera house are shattered by Allied bombing.

1963. Reopens on 22 November with Wagner's Die Meistersinger von Nürnberg. *The auditorium retains its original plan, and the grand staircase as well as the foyer have been restored to their 1825 state.*

When it comes to opera houses, Munich surely missed its greatest opportunity when, in the mid-1860s, it rejected the monumental theatre proposed by Gottfried Semper and Richard Wagner. As a result, Semper returned to seek his fortune in Dresden, where, to some degree, he would realize the broad outlines of his scheme, while Wagner found a home in Bayreuth and there built his dream auditorium (which, ironically, Munich would get in the form of a close copy, the Prinzregententheater, designed by Max Littmann at the beginning of the 20th century). The Bavarian capital had to make do with the theatre Maximilian I built for his subjects in 1818, a classical building immediately outside the Royal Palace and linked by a covered passage to the Court Theatre, a Rococo gem designed in the 1730s by the Walloon architect François Cuvilliés. For the big new theatre, Karl von Fischer, at the the King's request, looked to the Odéon in Paris and emphasized the neo-Greek aspect of his operatic Parthenon by capping the portico with a triangular pediment, over which loomed a second tympanum, this one filling the gable of the high ridge roof. Fischer would not have long to enjoy his achievement, since he died only two years after the theatre opened. Three years later, moreover, the theatre itself disappeared, consumed by flames. The King thereupon increased the beer tax to finance

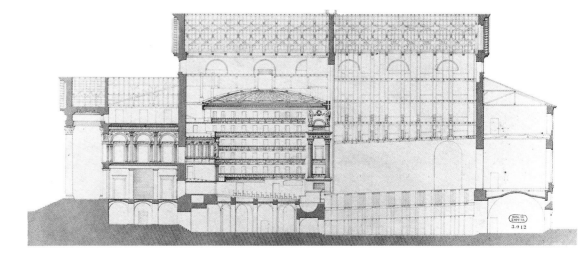

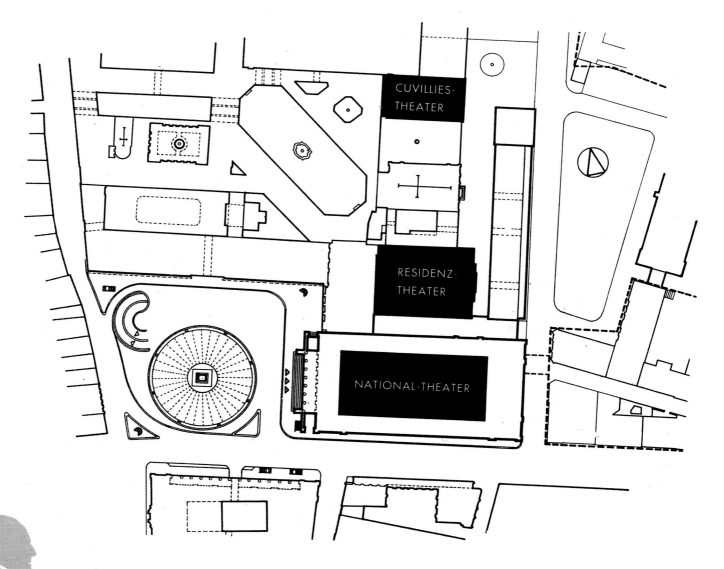

CUVILLIES-THEATER

RESIDENZ-THEATER

NATIONAL-THEATER

Munich has been a center of intense musical activity since the 15th century. **1653.** *The Court Opera, dedicated to the Italian repertory, is inaugurated. On its stage two of Mozart's operas receive their world premieres:* La Finta Giardiniera *(1775), an opera bouffe, and* Idomeneo, Re di Creta *(1781). Munich, the scene of many operatic premieres, earned its great musical fame through the privileged relations the city maintained with Mozart, Wagner, and Richard Strauss. Under the direction of Franz Lachner (1836-1868), Munich's opera house gave German opera—the works of Spohr, Marschner, Meyerbeer and Lortzing—a place alongside that of such Italian composers as Rossini and Verdi. The close ties between King Ludwig II and Richard Wagner transformed Munich, during the second half of the 19th century, into a Wagnerian stronghold, thus one of the centers of operatic life in Europe.*

reconstruction at the earliest possible moment, and assigned the job to Leo von Klenze. Klenze kept the main elements but departed somewhat from the original design by recasting all decorative features in the heavier Biedermeier style then popular. Reopened in 1825, the opera house remained blessedly untouched for almost a century before a new campaign of work got under way, modifying the access areas and enlarging the stage, which gained a turntable. By this time, however, dark political clouds were already gathering over Europe, and on 4 October 1943 Allied bombs fell on what was now the Bavarian State Opera. Not until twenty years later did the theatre rise anew, once more from the original Fischer plans. Although enlarged, the auditorium preserved its old quasi-circular shape, but the décor remained frozen in a pseudo-classical style. The grand staircase and the foyer were returned to their 1825 state. On the exterior, the upper pediment still displayed the polychrome design of old, but the one atop the portico recovered the paleness of stone. Backstage, the layout introduced in the 1930s continued in place, although slightly enlarged.

Ludwig II not only sponsored the premieres of Wagner's operas; he also insisted upon midnight performances, given for himself alone. Another requirement was that musicians and staff go about in house slippers so as not to disturb the audience of one with creaking steps on a parquet floor.

The operas of Richard Wagner premiered in Munich:

1865. Tristan und Isolde, *conducted on 10 June by Hans von Bülow, then still married to Cosima Liszt. Although divorced a year later, Cosima would not marry Wagner until 25 August 1870. Meanwhile, her daughter by Wagner— a child named Isolde—had been born during the same year as the opera.*

1868. Die Meistersinger von Nürnberg *on 21 June under the direction of Hans von Bülow.*

1869. Das Rheingold.

1870. Die Walküre.

1871. *Wagner decides to build a theatre at Bayreuth.*

1901. *Ernst von Possart establishes the Munich Festival.*

1919. *The era of Richard Strauss begins in Munich, following the premiere in Vienna of* Die Frau ohne Schatten. *Strauss was born in Munich in 1864, the son of a noted horn player employed at the Court Theatre. At the age of sixteen, he met Hans von Bülow, who introduced him to the music of Wagner. Strauss accepted the post of conductor at the opera house but then departed for Dresden, where he became Kapellmeister. For the years 1894-1898 Strauss returned to his native city, where he served as chief conductor. Two of his many operas would be premiered there:*

1938. Friedenstag.

1942. Capriccio.

After World War II, Munich continued to be one of Europe's operatic capitals, the quality of its productions and performances steadily maintained at a very high level. This success derives from the presence of both international stars and great German singers within the context of superb ensemble work.

World Premieres since 1945:

1956. *Henri Tomasi's* Miguel Mañara.

1957. *Paul Hindemith's* Die Harmonie der Welt.

1978. *Aribert Reimann's* Lear.

CUVILLIÉS THEATRE

This Rococo jewel was built between 1751 and 1753 by the Walloon architect François Cuvilliés the Elder, who began his career at the age of eight as court dwarf in the service of the Elector Maximilian II Emmanuel of Bavaria, a monarch with an eye for talent. Sent to Paris, Cuvilliés studied architecture under François Blondel, later famous as the teacher of François Ledoux, before returning to Munich, where he became court architect in 1725. During World War II, his Residenztheater was dismantled to save it from aerial bombardments. In 1956-1958 the masterpiece was reassembled on another site, the "pharmacy" wing of the Royal Palace, where it became the Cuvilliés Theatre. The new setting, made it possible for the little opera house to have a roomier stage and more accommodating stairs, as well as a vestibule almost as large as the auditorium.

FACT ABOUT THE BAVARIAN STATE OPERA BUILDING

1818 *Karl von Fischer, architect*
1825 *Leo von Klenze, architect*
1930 *Enlargement of the stage and the two side areas*
1963 *Gerhard Graaubner, architect working from the original plans by Karl von Fischer*

Horseshoe auditorium
Capacity: 2,100
1 orchestra stalls
5 balconies
1 gallery
Proscenium: **width** 15m; **height** 13m
Stage: **width** 27.60m; **height** 28.75m; **depth** 22.80m

FACTS ABOUT THE CUVILLIÉS THEATRE BUILDING

1753 *François Cuvilliés, architect*
1958 *Reassembled in the "pharmacy" wing of the Royal Palace*

Capacity: 523
Horseshoe auditorium
1 orchestra stalls
3 tiers of boxes
1 gallery
Proscenium: **width** 10.10m
Stage: **depth** 15.30m

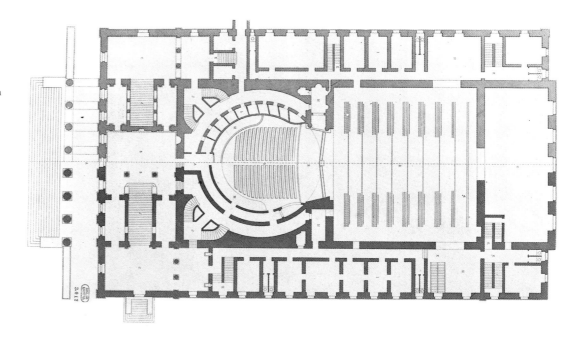

Teatro Colón
Buenos Aires

TEATRO COLÓN
Buenos Aires - Argentina

1856. *The first Teatro Colón is built, with 2,500 seats and a cazuela (a gallery reserved for women). It is inaugurated on 25 April 1857 with Verdi's* La Traviata.

1888. *The first Teatro Colón is demolished and the land sold for 950,000 pesos to the National Bank, which plans to establish its new headquarters on the site.*

1908. *The new Teatro Colón opens on 25 May with Verdi's* Aida, *following years of dispute. The project had also been troubled by the death of its chief architect, Francesco Tamburini, who was succeeded by his pupil, Victor Meano, himself struck down in 1904, this time by an assassin. Julio Dormal finally completed the Italian-style house.*

1966. *The ceiling over the auditorium is redecorated by Soldi.*

FACTS ABOUT THE BUILDING

1856 *The first Teatro Colón*
1889 *Francesco Tamburini and Angelo Ferrari, architects of the second Teatro Colón*
1904 *Victor Meano, architect*
1908 *Julio Dormal, architect*

Horseshoe auditorium
Capacity: 2,367, plus standing room for 1,000
Proscenium: **width** 16m; **height** 8.50m
Stage: width 20m; **height** 23m; **depth** 20m

When opera reached Buenos Aires in the 19th century it found a home in the modest Coliseo, which programmed a variety of works drawn from the Italian repertory. Gradually, foreign companies appeared offering Argentines a wider selection of operatic fare, first German and then French, the success of which persuaded the city to favor itself with a theatre worthy of the name. The first Teatro Colón opened in 1857 with a performance of *La Traviata*, only four years after the premiere of the Verdi opera in Venice. The new theatre, with its 2,500 seats, including a gallery reserved for women, very quickly emerged as the center of musical life in Buenos Aires and a source of pride for the young Argentine republic. But after thirty-five years of reliable service, the original Colón had become obsolete and was sold to the National Bank for a million pesos, a sum the municipality used to underwrite the erection of a venue both larger and equipped with the latest technology. The first stone was laid in 1889, to the accompaniment of a hymn specially composed for the occasion, but the event turned out to be no more than a prelude to a construction process that would drag on for twenty years, fraught the whole way with misadventures worthy of a soap opera. Quarrels among interested parties slowed down the enterprise, beginning with the choice of site at the center of Buenos Aires. Then, in 1903, events took a tragic turn when Francesco Tamburini, the principal architect, suddenly died. A year later, his assistant, Victor Meano, was murdered, which left Julio Dormal to bring the project to conclusion in 1908. On the exterior, the opera house is a gigantic pastiche, a sort of combination of Vienna's Staatsoper, Milan's La Scala, and the Palais Garnier in Paris. Inside, the opulence of the décor was, to say the least, exuberant and, for that reason, the delight of the public, which found accommodation in some 2,500 seats, plus room for another thousand spectators willing to stand just as audiences had done in the 18th century. Traditional in form and plan, the auditorium managed, despite its great size, to seem intimate, a feeling reinforced in the orchestra stalls by a dozen boxes screened for the benefit of families in mourning, who could thus enjoy the opera without appearing to flout social convention. Perfect acoustics and a large, well-equipped, functional stage soon made

1868. *Under the leadership of Angelo Ferrari, the Teatro Colón scales the heights in the world of Italian opera, its casts rivaling those at the Metropolitan or La Scala. Bizet's* Carmen *is performed by a French company.*

1888. *A great season featuring the fabled soprano Adelina Patti* (right).

1908. *The new Teatro Colón opens on 25 March with Verdi's* Aïda *before an audience of almost 4,000.*

1912. *Arturo Toscanini conducts the South American premiere of Paul Dukas's* Ariane et Barbe-Bleue, *to great critical and popular acclaim. His singers include such international stars as Lucrezia Bori, Giuseppe de Luca, and Nazzareno de Angelis. The maestro conducts his favorite works:* Tristan und Isolde, Aïda, Mefistofele, Manon Lescaut, *and* Falstaff.

1915. *Walter Mocchi is director until 1925, a period in which French opera would be favored.*

1927. *For the centenary of Beethoven's death, Teatro Colón schedules performances of all nine of the composer's symphonies.*

1931. *The theatre becomes municipal. Otto Klemperer conducts the last* Ring *cycle of his career.*

1936. *Igor Stravinsky conducts a long series of concerts.*

1940. *Arturo Toscanini, in flight from the Nazis, returns to Teatro Colón.*

1948. *Kirsten Flagstad, the celebrated Wagnerian soprano from Norway, makes her debut at Teatro Colón, as does the young Maria Callas. After 1949, financial difficulties during the Peron regime have an adverse effect on the artistic life of the Teatro Colón.*

1950-1960. *A period of great conductors at the Colón, including Sir Thomas Beecham, who conducts* The Magic Flute, Fidelio, Otello, Carmen, *and* Samson et Dalila.

1953. *Darius Milhaud's* Christophe Colomb. *Following the revolution of 1955, Teatro Colón recovers the artistic standards it had long known in the past.*

1964. *Premiere of Alberto Ginastera's* Don Rodrigo.

Adelina Patti (1843–1919).

the Teatro Colón, during the first decades of the 20th century, an operatic beacon whose seasons achieved a level of excellence comparable to those at the Metropolitan or La Scala. Toscanini, Beecham, Klemperer and Stravinksy all conducted here many times. In 1967 there were six complete cycles of Wagner's *Ring*. Since the 1970s, Teatro Colón has been a magnet for the world's greatest singers.

Grand-Théâtre
Geneva

1861. *The municipality of Geneva decides to build a new opera house.*
1872. *A competition for an opera house design is opened and the prize awarded by the jury to Émile Reverdin. In the end, however, the contract goes to a non-competitor, the architect Jacques-Élysée Goss.*
1874. *Construction is begun, financed by a legacy from Charles, Duke of Brunswick. The personifications of Tragedy, Dance, Music, and Comedy presiding over the grand staircase come from the studios of the sculptors Massaroti, Custor, Salmson, and Iquel. The materials used in the opera house*

Without Voltaire and his soirées at Ferney, Geneva's music lovers would never have known the delights of opera, an art form banned from the city by the puritanical legacy of Jean Calvin. It was only in 1766 that Geneva got its first theatre, La Grange aux Étrangers, built outside the walls. This venue would soon be replaced by the Théâtre de Neuve, it too situated on the promenade around the ramparts. In 1872 a legacy from the Duke of Brunswick made it possible to open a competition for a new opera house. However, instead of Émile Reverdin, the winner voted by the jury, the architect eventually chosen was Jacques-Élysée Goss, who produced nothing more than a pale copy of the Palais Garnier in Paris. The loggia across the façade, the dome crowning the auditorium, the roof over the stage building, and the lateral spaces—everything that contributed to the distinctive silhouette of the Paris Opera—could be found in Geneva, albeit on a reduced scale. On the interior, Goss relied more on his own resources, since he too was a winner of the Prix de Rome, and, without copying Paris's imperial pomp, gave the republicans of Geneva a foyer with a very grand set of staircases. When fire broke out in 1951, it provided an opportunity for the Grand-Théâtre to be reconstructed in a manner far removed from Garnier pastiche. In place of the half-dome followed by a ridge roof came an immense concrete sail billowing like an envelope right over both auditorium and stage building. The back of the structure was expanded, until it even encroached upon the Place Neuve, so as to create a German-style stage supplemented by side and back stages. As for the severely modern,

include red marble from Valais, gray sandstone from Saint Gallen, rock from the Jura, and molasse from Bern.

1879. *Inaugurated on 2 October with Rossini's* William Tell.

1951. *In May a fire breaks out, partially destroying the opera house, but leaving the walls and the foyer in a salvageable state. Reconstruction begins during the same year. The stage is enlarged in the German manner (1 backstage and 2 side stages for managing scenery). The auditorium is redesigned with two balconies and a steep top gallery formed like an amphitheatre. The original dome is replaced by an elliptical roof of concrete.*

1962. *The rebuilt Grand-Théâtre, though still under construction, reopens with Verdi's* Don Carlos.

1766. *Before the arrival of Voltaire, opera had never been performed in Geneva, thanks to the puritanical Reformation brought to the city in the 16th century by Jean Calvin. Voltaire, first at Délices and than at Ferney, became the first resident to organize operatic performances for the higher ranks of society.*

1767. *The Rosimond Theatre is inaugurated with Grétry's* Isabelle et Gertrude, *an opera with a libretto by Voltaire and Favart.*

Despite the arrival of the Grand-Théâtre in 1879, Geneva remains a relatively dim outpost in the world of opera for yet another century—with certain exceptions:

1892. *The world premiere of the French version of Jules Massenet's* Werther, *on 27 December.*

1912. *Ernest Ansermet conducts Debussy's* Palleas et Melisarde.

Since 1980, the Grand-Théâtre has become one of the leading opera houses of Europe, thanks to the quality of the Suisse Romande Orchestra, a wide-ranging repertory, and exceptional planning. The artistic policy of the house, which favors new works and productions over ongoing repertory, came from the director, Hugues Gall, who in 1995 assumed leadership of the Opéra National de Paris. In Geneva, Gall maintained the Italian stagione tradition of one carefully prepared opera running at a time. Some seasons, thanks to their sensational productions, have generated considerable excitement.

1980. On 11 September a new production of Mozart's Don Giovanni, starring Ruggiero Raimondi, is mounted with stage direction by Maurice Béjart and musical direction by Horst Stein. "I'm not trying to put myself into Mozart's work, where the composer has already put so much of himself, so that anything further would crush the work rather than illuminate it." With these words, the choreographer characterizes his approach to Don Giovanni; merely by interpreting he finds himself drawn into a very dark view of life. Thus, black is the color chosen for the sets, Raimondi's attire, the dark glasses, and even the costumes worn by the corps de ballet. On an empty stage purged of all the usual trappings, death stalks a production that leaves critics as well as the public in a state of shock.

1982. On 29 January Rolf Liebermann's new production of Wagner's Parsifal is staged, under the baton of Horst Stein. "To mount Parsifal in 1982 one must grasp the mythological thread with one hand and the futurist thread with the other, seize images that speak to us, that lodge in today's unconscious, the subliminal life of a world in the wake of Hiroshima," commented Liebermann about his first attempt at directing. Scenes from Alain Resnais' film projected on a stage backdrop, animated drawings by Christophe Vaillaux (representing a luxuriant garden), and the sets of Peterika Ionesco serve to revisualize the Wagnerian

wood-paneled auditorium, a steep, amphitheatre-like balcony now hangs above the orchestra stalls and the first two balconies, adding some three hundred seats to the theatre's overall capacity. Today, Calvin would have no choice but to admit defeat, for since the arrival of Hugues Gall in the 1980s, Geneva has become one of the great strongholds of opera in contemporary Europe.

Decorative painting and sculpture of 1874
which survived the fire of 1951.

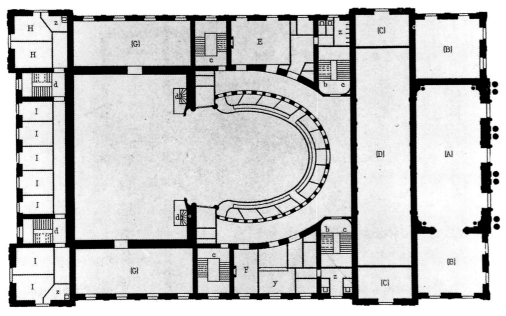

FACTS ABOUT THE BUILDING

1879 *Jacques-Élysée Goss, architect*
1962 *Marcello Zavelani-Rossi, Charles Shopfer, and
Jacek Stryjenski, architects*
Capacity: 1,500
Fan-shaped auditorium
3 tiers of balconies
Proscenium: **width** 18m; **height** 12m
Stage: **width** 18m; **height** 30m; **depth** 20m

universe in a very free, non-traditional manner, a vision steeped in the late-20th-century nightmare of a nuclear apocalypse.

1982. *The premiere on 19 December of a new production of Jacques Offenbach's* La Périchole, *directed by Jérôme Savary. Marc Soustrot conducts a cast headed by Neil Rosenshein, Gabriel Bacquier, and Ricardo Cassinelli.*

1984. *On 17 April Ken Russell offers his production of Rossini's* L'Italiana in Algeri, *performed under the baton of Myung-Whun Chung, who would soon become principal conductor at the new Opéra de la Bastille in Paris.*

1985. *Jérôme Savary's new production of Offenbach's* Voyage dans la lune *receives its first performance on 12 December, with a cast headed by Joseph Evans and Marie McLaughlin. World premiere on 18 April of Girolamo Arrigo's* Le Retour de Casanova, *directed by Jorge Lavelli, conducted by Reynald Giovaninetti, and sung by Scott Reeve and Fiorella Pediconi.*

Ballets Russes
The Russian avant-garde found an exceptionally loyal following in Geneva, where Diaghilev's Ballets Russes performed for the first time on 20 December 1915. The elite of Geneva filled the Grand-Théâtre for the event, proceeds from which went to Russian victims of World War I. The demand for tickets proved so great that hundreds of applicants had to be turned away. The program began with "God Save the Tsar," sung by the Wagnerian soprano Felia Litvinne. It then proceeded with the world premiere of Soleil de nuit, *a ballet choreographed by Leonide Massine, then a twenty-year-old prodigy. Igor Stravinsky was on the podium and Diaghilev in the wings.*

Alexandre Benois' sketch for the Chinese costume in Stravinsky's fairytale opera, *The Nightingale* (1913).

Mozart's *Don Giovanni*, produced by Maurice Béjart in 1973 with Ruggiero Raimondi (on the right) in the title role.

Národní Divadlo

Prague

1862. *The small Provisional Theatre, designed by Ignác Ullman, opens on National Avenue along the Vltava embankment.*

1866. *Josef Zitek wins the design competition sponsored by the Committee of Czech Patriots for a new opera house open to the general public.*

1868. *On May 1 the foundation stones are laid.*

1881. *Inaugurated on 11 June with Bedrich Smetana's* Libuse. *The new National Theatre boasts an imposing portico flanked by two recessed towers each surmounted by a bronze equestrian group. The attic is housed in*

The mighty House of Habsburg, exercising imperial power from its capital in Vienna, long made certain that German and Italian works prevailed on the operatic stages of Prague. By the mid-19th century, however, Czech opera was beginning to emerge, hand in hand with the rise of Bohemian nationalism. Finally, in 1862, after two decades of debate, the Diet of the Bohemian Estates authorized the construction of the small Provisional Theatre (Prozatímní Divadlo) on the banks of the Vltava (Moldau). But this was a mere beginning for Czech patriots, who had much grander things in mind, even though the German-dominated Estates refused to fund them. A competition judged by Eduard van der Nüll and August Siccard von Siccardsburg, architects of the Hofoper in Vienna, produced a winning design in the proposal submitted by one of their own pupils, Josef Zitek. By 1 May 1868 every province in the kingdom had sent a stone to be laid into the foundations of a monument viewed from the start as a symbol of national unity. A major challenge for Zitek was the wedge shape of the site, which required that he either extend along the river the lateral façade of the Provisional Theatre, a structure already contiguous with other buildings, or invent a series of tricky setbacks that would allow a proper entrance

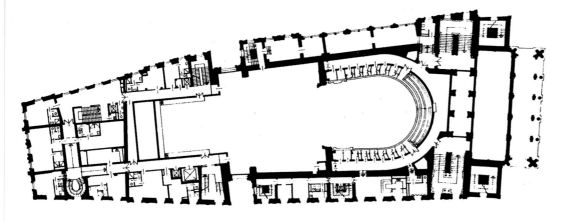

without overwhelming the little square on to which it would give. As in Budapest, the National Theatre, apart from a few murals dedicated to Czech identity, yielded to the contemporary passion for the Italian Renaissance. The new house opened on 11 June 1881 with the world premiere of Smetana's *Libuse*. Two months later, on 12 August, flames reduced it to ashes. It is a measure of the Praguers' feelings that within forty-seven days they had raised enough money to rebuild. The event proved

a lapis-blue, star-studded imperial roof, its humped mass culminating in a platform rimmed about by a gilded fretwork railing. In the auditorium, the royal box at the center of the horseshoe embodies the hope that one day Bohemia would have its own king. The Neo-Renaissance décor is the work of the first generation of artists dedicated to Bohemian nationalism: the painter Mikulás Ales and the sculptors Josef Myslbek, Bohuslav Schnirch, and Antonín Wagner.

1881. *Fire breaks out on 12 August after only eleven performances, destroying the auditorium, the stage, and the ceilings. Josef Schulz, Zitek's pupil, undertakes to rebuild the opera house.*

1883. *The National Theatre reopens, with the Provisional Theatre now absorbed into the whole. Again, Smetana's* Libuse *is performed.*

1983. *Pavel Kupka and then Karel Progner erect three new buildings—all severely modern glass boxes—on the urban side of the National Theatre, housing a multipurpose auditorium, a restaurant, and technical services.*

Richard Strauss, by Wilhelm Viktor Krauss.

FACTS ABOUT THE BUILDING

1881 *Josef Zitek, architect*
1883 *Josef Schulz, architect*
1978 *Bohuslav Fuchs, architect*
1983 *Pavel Kupka followed by Karel Progner, architects*
U-shaped auditorium
Capacity: 1,554 seats
3 tiers of boxes, 2 balconies, 2 galleries
Proscenium: **width** 11.60m; **height** 9.70m
Stage: **width** 21m; **height** 11m; **depth** 20m

especially tragic for Zitek, since it cast so many doubts on his plans that he had to resign in favor of one of his own pupils, Josef Schulz. This architect lengthened the auditorium, gutted the Provisional Theatre to create rehearsal halls and put offices in the adjoining houses. On the exterior, Schulz harmonized the façades over which now rose the massive imperial roof of the theatre proper. On 18 November 1883 the rebuilt opera house opened, with *Libuse* once again on the stage. A century later to the day, Smetana's patriotic opera, long identified with the revival of Czech culture, would serve anew to crown a building campaign at the opera house, this one delayed by the insurrection of 1968. The restoration included the addition of a backstage, followed by a new lateral wing, a commission given first to Pavel Kupka and then to Karel Progner, who designed three ultra-modern glass boxes housing the multipurpose New Stage auditorium, a restaurant, and technical services, on a site where Zitnek's splendid loggia once looked upon nothing but a dark lane.

Joan Rodgers in Mozart's *Marriage of Figaro*, produced by Giorgio Strehler.

The Nostic or Tyl Theatre:

1783. *Built by Count Nostic, the theatre opens.*

1786. *Mozart conducts* The Marriage of Figaro *shortly after the opera's premiere in Vienna.*

1787. *The triumphant world premiere on 29 October of Mozart's* Don Giovanni, *conducted by the composer himself.*

1791. *The premiere of Mozart's* La Clemenza di Tito, *commissioned by the Prague municipality.*

1798. *The Nostic becomes the Royal Estates or National Theatre.*

1813-1816. *Carl Maria von Weber is director of the Theatre.*

1949. *The Estates Theatre is renamed the Tyl Theatre by the Communist regime.*

Bedrich Smetana *(1824-1884). Aided by Franz Liszt and Clara Schumann, Smetana launched the Czech school of nationalist music in 1849. In 1862 he took charge of the orchestra at the new Provisional Theatre. It was for this venue that Smetana composed his principal operas:* The Bartered Bride *(1866),* The Brandenburghers in Bohemia *(1866),* Dalibor *(1868), and* Libuse *(1881).*

Antonín Dvorák *(1841-1904). Dvorák wrote his New World Symphony in New York, where he was director of the National Conservatory. In 1901 he returned to Prague and took up a similar post, while continuing to compose and conduct.*

Below: the Nostic (or Tyl) Theatre, in Prague, where Mozart's *Don Giovanni* was first performed on 29 October, 1787, under the baton of the composer.

Above: detail from the ceiling painting of the Národní Theatre, Prague.

The auditorium of the Národní Theatre, Prague.

Magyar Állami Operaház *Budapest*

1873. *A competition for a new theatre design is won by Miklós Ybl, a Hungarian architect trained in Vienna.*
1874. *Franz Joseph I, Habsburg Emperor of the Austro-Hungarian Empire, finances the construction of the Budapest Imperial Opera (Operaház).*
1884. *Inaugurated on 27 September with Act I of Wagner's* Lohengrin, *followed by Act I of Ferenc Erkel's* Bánk Bán, *conducted by the composer, before an audience that includes the Emperor*

From its late-18th-century origins in the theatre in the Castle, the history of Hungarian opera has been little more than one long struggle for national identity against cultural domination by the Habsburg empire governing from Vienna. The threat loomed even larger after the German Theatre was inaugurated in 1812. A quarter of a century later, however, the Hungarian cause found revived hope in the Theatre of Pest, which opened in 1837 and began programming the operas of its Hungarian director, Ferenc Erkel, as well as such standard repertory as Rossini's *Barber*. The company moved into the new Operaház in 1884. Here, although the repertory would, for the most part, be sung in Hungarian (a practice that could only encourage the development of national opera) it still represented a sort of peaceful co-existence between a Hungarian-language dramatic theatre, proud of its hard-won autonomy, and the operatic theatre, dependent upon the patronage of the Austrian ruling class. To complicate matters further, Emperor Franz Joseph appointed as director of the Budapest Imperial Opera none other than Gustav Mahler, himself a Hungarian and well known in the Magyar world but educated and trained in Vienna. The competition for the new Operaház announced in 1873 was won by Miklós Ybl with a design which was clearly a bid for international recognition and which was inspired by whatever was most successful at the time. From the Palais Garnier he took the loggia as well as the form of the foyer and its grand staircase; from Vienna he appropriated the recessed attic supporting one continuous roof over both auditorium and stage; and from Dresden he adopted the Neo-Renaissance deco-

Franz Joseph I. The Operaház becomes the most important lyric theatre in Hungary. Decorated in the manner of the Italian Renaissance, the interior features murals by Kovács, Székely, Vastagh, Lotz, and Than. For the first time anywhere, the stage is equipped with a revolutionary hydraulic system (the Asphaleia system, designed by the engineer Robert Gewinner) making it possible to raise, lower, or tilt the stage.
1945. *The Operaház, now the Magyar Allami Operaház, reopens at the end of the World War II, during which it suffered only slight damage.*
1979. *Complete restoration is begun, involving a team of East German engineers, who replace the Asphaleia system with an electrical one.*
1984. *The Operaház resumes performances following a five-year closure.*

1888. *Gustav Mahler, the principal conductor until 1891, adds a number of German works to the repertory. He is succeeded, in 1893-1895, by Arthur Nikisch, who concentrates on Italian, French, and Hungarian works. Soon thereafter the Operaház enters a relatively calm period, which lasts until 1913. The company is then led by Miklós Bánffy, with Egisto Tango on the podium until 1919.*

Gustav Mahler (1860–1911).

1915. *The Operaház presents the works of Hungarian composers including Zóltan Kodály (1882-1967), despite the outbreak of World War I and some public resistance.*

FACTS ABOUT THE BUILDING

1884 *Miklós Ybl, architect*
1984 *Complete renovation*

Capacity: 2400
Horseshoe auditorium
3 tiers of boxes and 1 gallery
Proscenium: **width** 14m; **height** 10m
Stage: **width** 28m; **height** 26m; **depth** 25m

1918. *The premiere on 24 May of* Bluebeard's Castle, *a 1-act opera by Belá Bartók, seven years after its composition. This is the only opera in the whole of the Hungarian master's large œuvre.*

1926. *The premiere on 16 October of* Háry János, *an operatic "fable" in 3 acts by Zóltan Kodály, who composed two other works for the stage:* Székely fonó *(1924) and* Czinka Panna *(1948), a history play in the form of a* Singspiel. *After 1945, Russian operas enter the repertory for the first time.*

1947. *Otto Klemperer, who had to leave Berlin in 1933, succeeds Ferenc Fricsay as music director.*

rative style. On the façade, finally, Ybl mixed all these influences into a stylistic salad entirely his own. For the auditorium he allowed the Italian plan to prevail, complete with three rings of boxes and a top gallery. The only original aspects are the slightly stepped-back alignment of the rising tiers and the obsequious convergence of the sight lines onto the imperial boxes. Ybl displayed his ingenuity on the stage, where he installed hydraulic machinery, a new technology that greatly reduced the risk of fire, while permitting all or part of the stage to move with unprecedented ease. Having escaped major damage during World War II, the Operaház quickly resumed its regular schedule of activities, until 1979, when it underwent major renovation. Fortunately, this did not impair the theatre's *Mitteleuropa* charm, most notable in the galleries and intimate little wood-paneled salons surrounding the grand foyer.

Detail of fresco in Renaissance style, 1884.

Teatro Amazonas
Manaus, Brazil

1881. *The rubber barons of Amazonas recommend the construction of a theatre, and the provincial government agrees.*
1896. *Inaugurated on 31 December with excerpts from Italian operas.*
1901. *The theatre is decorated, under the direction of Crispin de Amoral.*
1929. *Reconstruction.*
1974. *Restoration.*
1990. *Teatro Amazonas reopens following three years of rehabilitation needed to save it from the adverse effects of humidity.*

FACTS ABOUT THE BUILDING

capacity: 1,600
1896 *Domenico de Angelis, architect*
1974 *Renato Braga, architect*
1929, 1965, 1990 *Restorations*

*I*n spite of Werner Herzog's film *Fitzcarraldo*, Iquitos is not Manaus, the voice of Caruso was never heard ringing through the virgin forest, Pavlova never risked her points on such rough terrain and no riverboat was portaged over the Amazonian hills to deliver supplies to the work site. Nevertheless, the actual story of how the Teatro Amazonas came into being is almost as incredible. In late-19th-century Manaus, opera existed in theatres that were modest at best, the sort of places that one day would become cinemas. The wealthy, however, dreamt of more spectacular productions as well as grandiose foyers in which to display their newly acquired wealth. Most of all, they longed for a proper auditorium comparable to those in the Old World. In 1881, therefore, it was the rubber barons themselves who persuaded the provincial government to build a theatre worthy of their ambitions. Construction got under way shortly thereafter, but it would take more than fifteen years just to complete the exterior. The plans came from a firm of architects in Lisbon, and they called for a resolutely Neoclassical façade, which would shift towards Art Deco by the time they reached the dome. Another five years passed before the interior could be fully decorated, under the supervision of Crispin de Amoral, an artist active in the Old World as well as in the New. The woods came from the forest of Amazonia, the stone from Portugal, the marbles, mosaics, and chandeliers from Venice, and the wrought iron, the clocks, and the trompe-l'oeil murals from Paris. As for the paintings on canvas applied to the interior of the dome, they originated in Italy, which earned the auditorium the name of "the Little Scala." Unfortunately, the Manaus Opera had scarcely been inaugurated when it had to curtail performances in 1907, owing to the collapse of the rubber market. During this century the Amazonian jungle has been opened up by improved roads and air transport, but Manaus is still one of the most remote places in the world. The maintenance of an opera house in these conditions was not easy. Between 1929 and 1974 several attempts were made to restore the house, some of them with unhappy results, especially in the foyer and the top gallery. The stage also underwent modernization. Only at the end of the 1980s, however, following eight decades of silence, did

Beginning in the late 19th century, Teatro Amazonas offered a series of Italian seasons, playing regular host to the Compagnia Lirica Italiana, which, together with Fernandez de Carvalho, staged performances of La Bohème, Rigoletto, Il Trovatore, Un Ballo in Maschera, Aida, *and* Il Barbiere di Siviglia.

1901. *The same company presents Carlos Gomes's* Il Guarany, *following performances in Milan and Rio. In September a zaegue company arrives, under the leadership of the Mexican impresario Gustavo de Maria Campos, bringing with it a repertory of 28 zarzuelas, 4 operettas, and 4 operas (including a new one: Arrieta's* Marina).

The Amazonas Opera boasts a roster of 19 soloists, a 32-member chorus, and an orchestra with 16 musicians. To the 6 operas cited above, the company adds Ernani, Faust, *and Gomes's* Fosca, *as well as a repertory of 10 operettas. Until 1907 the house offers a mixed program of operas and concerts while also presenting celebrated artists from abroad.*

1907. *The first performances in Amazonas of Donizetti's* La Favorita, *Meyerbeer's* L'Africaine, *and Halévy's* La Juive.

1909-1937. *Only performances by touring companies are scheduled.*

Carlos Gomes *(1836-1896), the Brazilian composer, studied in Milan from 1864 to 1866, before going on to found a Portuguese opera house in Rio de Janeiro.*

His operatic works include:

1861. A Noite do Castelo.

1870. Il Guarany, *premiered at La Scala in Milan on 19 March.*

1889. O Escravo (Lo Schiavo), *first performed in Rio de Janeiro.*

1891. Candor, *premiered at La Scala.*

1990. *On 17 March the Teatro Amazonas reopens with an all-Brazilian program, which includes excerpts from Gomes's* Lo Schiavo *and* Il Guarany. *An international season follows, commencing on 29 March with a performance of Bizet's* Carmen.

the Manaus Opera come back to life following a new round of restoration, this time of the highest quality. The work involved a battle to overcome hostile nature, in a country where it rains 165 days a year, where a piano needs nine months of treatment to protect it against the climate, and where it took fourteen months of struggle and sixteen tons of insecticide to eliminate the termites threatening the structure. As if to prove that legends always have a basis in reality, Manaus could finally boast that its reopening was graced by the presence of an illustrious tenor and a great ballerina: Placido Domingo and Marcia Haydée.

Teatro Municipal
Rio de Janeiro and São Paulo

TEATRO MUNICIPAL
Rio de Janeiro and São Paulo, Brazil

1909. Rio de Janeiro. *Inaugurated on 14 July 1909 with the national anthem, leaving a full season to begin only in 1910.*
1911. São Paulo. *Inaugurated on 12 September with Ambroise Thomas's* Hamlet *sung in Italian.*

FACTS ABOUT THE BUILDING: SÃO PAULO

1911 *Arthur Ramos de Azevedo, architect*
Capacity: 1750
1 orchestra stalls, 3 balconies, 1 gallery
Proscenium: **width** 12.30m; **height** 7m
Stage: **width** 18m; **depth** 25m

Rio de Janeiro flirted with opera as early as the late 18th century, and the colonial city even saw a minor flowering of the art after 1807, when the Portuguese court arrived in exile from the Napoleonic wars, but not until 1870 did opera take hold in São Paulo, the wealthy industrial and financial center of Brazil. By this time South America's largest country could benefit from the convergence of talents towards Teatro Colón in Buenos Aires. It was even in Rio that Toscanini wielded a baton for the first time in his career. And just as Buenos Aires prepared for the new century by building a vast new opera house, so Rio and São Paulo also launched into ambitious urbanistic schemes in which the keystone of each would be a large municipal theatre. In both cities, the planners very candidly took Second Empire Paris as their model, complete with noble façades lining wide avenues laid out star-burst fashion to provide long perspective views towards a climactic monument: the opera house. In Rio, things evolved as a family affair, beginning with the mayor, Francesco Pereira Passos, who, proud of his abilities as an engineer, took personal charge of his city's renewal. Meanwhile, his son, Francesco Oliveira Passos, won out over a French architect in the competition for a new lyric theatre, with a proposal that was nothing more than a clever pastiche of the Palais Garnier. Opened in 1909, the building shamelessly displays its loyalty to the Beaux-Arts tradition of France, from the overall silhouette to the paintings in the foyer. In São Paulo as well, the officials were scrupulous in their exploitation of Haussmannian urbanism, making the opera house the symbolic center of the projected new quarters. The commission for the theatre went to a triumvirate of architects—Ramos de Azevedo and Claudio and Domiziano Rossi—who also evinced a taste for that

Façade of the Teatro Municipal, Rio de Janiero.

Grand staircase of the Teatro Municipal, Rio de Janiero.

SÃO PAULO

1873. *The Teatro Provisório launches an Italian season on 20 August with Verdi's* Attila *and* Luisa Miller *and Donizetti's* Poliuto.

1876. *The San José Theatre presents Donizetti's* Lucia di Lammermoor, *Marchetti's* Ruy Blas, *and Petrella's* Jone.

1880. *The Ferrari company offers a season featuring Meyerbeer's* Les Huguenots *(in Italian) and Gomes's* Il Guarany *and* Fosca.

1881. *Opera in French for the first time: Thomas's* Mignon *and Bizet's* Carmen.

1882-1883. *Ferrari schedules a season of six operas, opening with Verdi's* Ernani *and closing with Bellini's* La Sonnambula. *Led by João Barbero, the company also becomes the pride of São Paulo by introducing Gomes's* Salvator Rosa. *In 1889,* Lo Schiavo, *one of the composer's last works, proves enormously successful with the public.*

1911. *Wagner is attempted for the first time, an initiative that leads two years later to performances of* Parsifal *and* Die Walküre, *sung in Italian. In the 1920s the operas were given in German as well, with* Die Meistersinger *and* Siegfried *added to the repertory. The 20th century would also bring the premieres of major operas by Brazilian composers: Campos's* A Bela Adormecida *(1924), Gome de Araújo's* Maria Petrowna *among them. The 1930s unfold as a Golden Age of opera in São Paulo.*

Arturo Toscanini *(1867-1957). It was in Rio, on 30 June 1886, that Toscanini first conducted an orchestra, for a memorable performance of* Aida, *following the departure of a maestro booed by the public. His stunning success prompted the impresario to place him in charge of all twelve of the other operas planned for the tour. An incomparable opera conductor, Toscanini presided over a number of historic premieres:* La Bohème *(Puccini) in 1896,* La Fanciulla del West *(Puccini) in 1910,* Nerone *(Boito) in 1925,* Turandot *(Puccini) in 1926 . . . . He served as principal conductor at La Scala in 1898-1903, at the Metropolitan Opera in 1908-1915, and again at La Scala in 1920-1929.*

Façade of the Teatro Municipal, São Paulo.

cocktail of Neoclassical and Renaissance elements, laced with a bit of Greco-Roman, which was the glory of the Garnier style. High-mindedness even held sway at the inauguration in 1911, when the house opened with a performance of Ambroise Thomas's *Hamlet.* Inside, Carrara marbles were de rigueur, as in Paris, but deployed with a certain Italian flair, thanks to Claudio Rossi. In the auditorium, which lost most of its boxes in the 1950s, the urban gamble paid off: the "coffee aristocracy" delighted at last to flaunt their wealth in a setting as opulent as those in the Old World. The singers, meanwhile, played to the gallery, packed with immigrants eager to catch even a few bars of music reminiscent of their native lands.

Auditorium of the Teatro Municipal, São Paulo.

Municipal Theatre *Hanoi*

MUNCIPAL THEATRE
Hanoi - Vietnam

1911. *Inaugurated.*

*I*n 1873 the tricolore flew over Hanoi, the city having been conquered by a French sailor, who went on to lose his life in a fight with Chinese pirates. His name, prophetically, was Garnier. Fifteen years later, France extended the protectorate throughout Indochina and colonial architecture proliferated more or less everywhere, its presence a symbol of overlord power as well as an expression of nostalgia for the mother country. In 1889 construction began on an opera house for Hanoi, a theatre that emerged as a scaled-down version of the Palais Garnier. Completed only in 1911, the building replicates, point for point, the model in Paris, from the broad steps of the portico to the attic balustrade, from the lateral pavilions to the roof over the stage building. Only the absence of a dome atop the auditorium made the copy look different from its prototype. Within the auditorium as well Garnier was the source, especially for the giant double columns rising through the tiers to support an entablature around the base of the circular ceiling. However, in its journey from the French Academy in Rome to a Tonkinese outpost, the Second Empire style shed many of its flourishes, arriving in a purified form innocent of the opulence so lavishly bestowed upon the Palais Garnier by relays of painters and decorators. As incongruous as an Eiffel Tower in the middle of a rice paddy, the Hanoi Opera House would nonetheless survive the departure of the French as well as the arrival of the Americans, and even the reunification of Vietnam, albeit caught in a process of slow disintegration. Today, it is merely a neglected municipal theatre where the roof leaks like a sieve and musicians perform under umbrellas during monsoonal downpours. Now, on the eve of the nation's third millennium, the Vietnamese government proposes to rebuild the Hanoi Opera House, with the help of France, turning it into an object of national pride, a monument freshly returned to its colonial splendor. It is hard to avoid a sense of irony.

V Twentieth-Century Variations

Opéra Municipal
Marseilles

OPÉRA MUNICIPAL
Marseilles - France

1787. The Parisian architect Bénard wins the commission for the Opéra de Marseille (Grand-Théatre or Salle Beauvau), which opens on 31 October with Tartuffe, *a 1-act play be Ponteuil, and Champein's* Mélomanie. *The theatre boasts a Neoclassical façade and a 2,000-seat auditorium modeled on Victor Louis' plan for Bordeaux.*

1919. On 13 November a fire destroys the Salle Beauvau. Ebrard, Castel, and Raymond, the architects in charge of the restoration, preserve the original stone colonnade and shell. In the entrance hall, the oak box office is placed at the center of a Venetian mosaic and framed on either side with two panels painted by Jean Jullien. At either end of the hall a grand staircase with wrought-iron railings leads up to the main foyer, a space embellished with an exotic-wood parquet, mahogany benches, gilt-iron sconces, a ceiling painted by Carrera, and marbles from Portugal.

In the 1,800-seat auditorium, the forestage boxes, the downstairs ring of boxes, the balcony, the galleries, and the gods are distinguished from one another by friezes of various designs. The gilded proscenium is capped with a bas-relief created by the sculptor Émile-Antoine Bourdelle. The great, uninterrupted expanse of the stage building was made possible by the technology of reinforced concrete.

As early as 1685 Marseilles was granted the privilege of opening an opera house in a tennis court. Not until 1787, however, did France's third largest city, after Paris and Lyons, erect its first true theatre, which rose on the site of an ancient arsenal where galleys had once been built. Bénard, the architect, who came from Paris, would have to contend with a somewhat turbulent local boy, Charles Ledoux, but in the end he won over the Academy, the academicism of his proposal being impeccable and his auditorium clearly inspired by the Bordeaux model of Victor Louis. A century later the Grand-Théâtre, or Salle Beauvau, was wired for electricity, which proved fatal. On 13 November 1919 a short circuit sparked a fire that spared nothing but the walls and the library. The task of reconstruction fell to a trio of architects, Ebrard, Castel, and Raymond, who salvaged only the façade and its classical portico, behind which they used reinforced concrete and marble to create an Art Deco temple, opened in 1924 as the Opéra Municipal de Marseille. The tone is set at the entrance colonnade culminating in an attic ornamented with four bas-reliefs of fauns frolicking *à l'antique.* Another bravura passage is Bourdelle's brick-red frieze on

a gold ground above the stage narrating the birth of beauty. Allegories from Greco-Roman antiquity also abound, from the staircases—avalanches of marble, stucco work, and bronze—to the foyer ceiling painted by Carrera. The auditorium, which has a conventional plan, three set-back balconies with undulating fronts, and a color scheme of pink, maroon, and gold, is a soul mate of the Théâtre des Champs-Élysées in Paris. Where Marseilles' Municipal Theatre differs is in its

1924. *The new opera house—the Opéra Municipal de Marseille—is inaugurated on 4 December with Reyer's* Sigurd, *the cast headed by Georges Cazenave, Mathilde Comes, Roumans, and Jacqueline Rouvier under the baton of Ferdinand Rey. For this exceptional evening, the audience was drawn by lots from the voter-registration lists, which left the mayor and his team to sit in the gallery.*

1972. *Marseilles' opera house undergoes a new restoration, at the end of which it reopens with a performance of Verdi's* Simon Boccanegra.

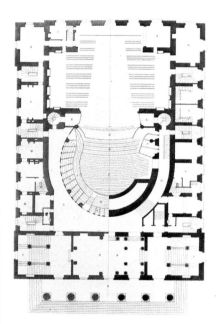

FACTS ABOUT THE BUILDING

1787 *Bénard, architect*
1924 *Ebrard, Castel, and Raymond, architects*

Capacity: 1,800
Urn-shaped auditorium
3 tiers of forestage boxes
1 ring of downstairs boxes
2 deep balconies
1 top gallery
Proscenium: **width** 11.50m; **height** 6.70-8m
Stage: **width** 14m; **height** 19.70m; **depth** 11.50m

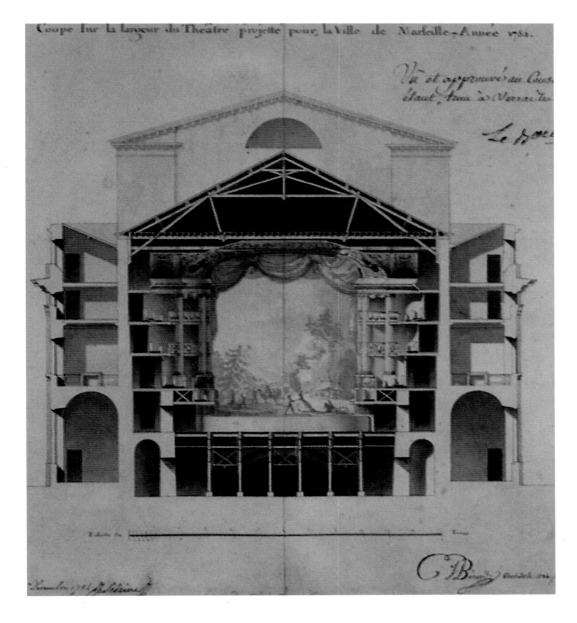

exuberance, from the festoons on the luminous crown and the curious garland of the lower boxes to the kitsch of the crenelated, "moderne" towers housing the front boxes. Outside, the theatre, unlike 19th-century prototypes, makes no attempt to conceal its internal functions. Surging above the mosaic-faced lateral façades—punctuated with trompe-l'oeil windows, real openings, and emergency exits—is the exposed, brutalist superstructure of a generously scaled stage building, its great span made possible by reinforced-concrete beams. However, the epicenter of the Municipal Theatre, which was restored in 1972, remains the top gallery, where a throng of regulars never hesitate to make their opinions known. It was here, furthermore, that the Mayor of Marseilles made the symbolic gesture of taking a seat in 1924 for the inauguration, marked by a performance of Reyer's *Sigurd*. And still today it is here that the success or failure of a work and its interpreters is decided.

1685. *Marseilles receives permission from Louis XIV to build an opera house. It opens with* Le Triomphe de la paix *by the Provençal composer Gautier, who was licensed to work for Marseilles, Toulouse, and Montpellier.*

1789. *Marseilles' Grand-Théâtre quickly becomes a popular rendezvous for intrigues and love-affairs. The slightest political innuendo from the stage triggers an open confrontation between royalists and nationalists. In September 1791, during the height of the Terror, royalists respond en masse to* Vive le Roi! *shouted by one of the singers in Monsigny's* Déserteur *based on a libretto by Sedaine. Republicans in the orchestra stalls thereupon cry* Vive la Nation! *During the same year, following the royal family's arrest at Varennes, a performance of Gluck's* Alceste *is curtailed when the numerous lines flattering Louis XIV prompt the audience to sing* Ça ira! *The Grand-Théâtre is renamed the Brutus and transformed into a place for commemorating great moments of the Revolution. A free performance is given on every tenth day of the ten-day week (in the Revolutionary calendar). Under the Napoleonic Empire, however, the Grand-Théâtre enters a period marked by great opulence.*

1858. *Beginning this year, Jacques Offenbach conducts several of his one-act operettas. Later, Verdi would triumph with* Il Trovatore *and* Rigoletto *(the title role of the latter sung in 1860 by the famous baritone Ismaël).*

1863. *Gounod's* Faust *is performed fourteen times during the season, with the Marseillaise soprano Marie Miolan-Carvalho in the role of Marguerite.*

1866. *The great Adelina Patti performs in* Lucia di Lammermoor *and* Il Barbiere di Siviglia. *Such is her success that for the second opera the price of a seat in the orchestra stalls rises from 15 francs to 60.*

1867. *Victor Maurel's performance in Rossini's* William Tell *makes a resounding impression.*

1871. *The Grand-Théâtre reopens after the Commune uprising. The city of*

Marseilles repurchases the opera house for 1,200,000 francs. The theatre's famously demanding audience has the power to send packing any singer not to its taste. Thus, when the tenor Montbert, a one-time cooper, intones "My God, what shall I do?" in the fourth act of Meyerbeer's Les Huguenots, *he finds himself quickly advised from the stalls: "Go back to your hogsheads!"*

Marseilles' opera house staged the French premieres of many famous works, including: Aida *in 1877, performed 25 times in three months; Giordano's* Fedora *in 1907; Massenet's* Don Quichotte *in 1910; Puccini's* La Fanciulla del West *in 1912; Mascagni's* Iris *in 1911. On one historic occasion in 1890 the great Australian soprano Nellie Melba sang the role of Ophelia in Ambroise Thomas's* Hamlet.

1963. *Berg's* Lulu.

1965. *Britten's* The Turn of the Screw.

1967. *Bennett's* The Mines of Sulphur.

1968. *Bibalo's* Le Sourire au pied de l'échelle *and Janáček's* The Makropoulos Case.

1971. *Menotti's* Maria Golovin.

1972. *Penderecki's* The Devils of Loudun.

1974. *Bentoiu's* Hamlet.

1975. *Rosenfeld's* Miracle à la cour.

1982. *Dvořák's* Rusalka.

1984. *Milhaud's* Christophe Colomb.

A number of famous contemporary singers have had their triumphant French debuts at Marseilles: Alfredo Kraus, Placido Domingo, and Renata Scotto among them.

Placido Domingo as Don José in Bizet's *Carmen.*

OPERA · MVNICIPAL

The Civic Opera House *Chicago*

THE CIVIC OPERA HOUSE

Chicago - United States

1929. *Inaugurated 4 December with Verdi's* Aida.

1993. *A radical overhaul of the backstage involves not only the machinery but also the creation of a new rehearsal hall the size of the actual stage. Updating extends to lighting, the hydraulic, mechanical, and electrical systems, the ventilation and the air-conditioning. By the time the dressing rooms and work spaces are renovated, the total cost comes to $100 million.*

A boomtown born in 1833, Chicago had to build opera houses on the scale of its skyscrapers. In 1865, the community which had yet to become America's Second City already boasted a 3,000-seat auditorium in a building that also housed galleries, offices, and studios. For a festival some twenty-five years later, an army of carpenters built a temporary wooden theatre blessed with thrilling acoustics, perfect sightlines, and elegant seats. Here an audience of 6,000 gathered to applaud Adelina Patti, all well protected from the rigors of winter by a central-heating system worked by steam. The success of that occasion prompted a group of financiers to commission the firm of Adler and Sullivan, then Chicago's most prestigious architects, to design an auditorium capable of satisfying the public's huge appetite for music and theatre. Opened in 1889, the neo-Romanesque Auditorium Building designed by Louis Sullivan incorporated an opera house, a 400-room hotel, and dozens of offices. With its 17-story tower, crowned with a water tank to feed the hydraulic stage machinery, Sullivan's masterpiece was the tallest structure in Chicago, as well as the most costly, and it remains one of the world's most massive. The opera house, which could accommodate an audience of 4,200 or 1,000 guests at a banquet, had a metal skeleton, cast-metal balcony fronts, air-conditioning, a fully articulated stage, and more than 5,000 electric lights lodged in a vast sunburst vault, whose elliptical shape, unfortunately, did not yield the very best acoustics. The Chicago Symphony would never play there, but operatic performances fared well enough. By 1925, however, Samuel Insull, a public-utilities magnate who presided over the affairs of the Chicago Civic Opera, had grown weary of Sullivan's opera house, deeming it obsolete, and set his sights on a new theatre. This time it seemed perfectly natural that Chicago, birthplace of the modern skyscraper,

After many years of financial instability, Chicago Lyric Opera, under the management of Ardis Krainik and the artistic direction of Bruno Bartoletti, has become one of the world's best-managed and most artistically secure companies. Lyric Opera is famous not only for the major singers who have made their American debuts there—Maria Callas for example—but also for the number of American or world premieres staged in the house, among them: Giannini's The Harvest (1961), Penderecki's Paradise Lost (1978), and Bolcom's McTeague (1992).

FACTS ABOUT THE BUILDING

1929 *Graham, Anderson, Probst, and White, architects*
1955 *A major campaign of restoration*
1993 *The backstage facilities enlarged to include a vast new rehearsal hall*
Fan-shaped auditorium
Capacity: 3,563
31 boxes; 3 balconies
Proscenium: **width** 16.20m; **height** 11.30m
Stage: **width** 40.50m; **height** 47m; **depth** 24.30m

would ignore European models and build its new opera house within a 46-story tower, designed by local architects and completed in 1929, the year of the Crash. The Chicago Civic Opera clearly symbolized a generation unburdened by tradition, and indeed it was conceived as a corporation in a building where numerous commercial spaces would subsidize the performing arts. A true people's house perhaps, but the Civic Opera nevertheless took care to impress its richest benefactors, dressing the vestibule and foyer in Roman marble, installing bronze doors, hanging chandeliers of Austrian crystal, and reveting the auditorium in solid oak. Orchestra stalls, some thirty boxes, and two levels of balcony provided seating for 3,563. As for the stage, it positively glistened with the latest in lighting and machinery. Time, however, catches up even with those who defy the heavens, and by 1993 the Chicago Lyric Opera, the resident company since 1956, found that it needed to enlarge its backstage facilities, a project that finally cost millions of dollars. It required purchasing substantial amounts of additional space in order to create a rehearsal hall and storage, while also refurbishing both the technical equipment and providing dressing rooms equal to the demands of today's divas.

War Memorial Opera House *San Francisco*

WAR MEMORIAL OPERA HOUSE
San Francisco - United States

1932. *Inaugurated 15 October with Puccini's* Tosca *featuring Claudia Muzio in the title role. The silhouette of the opera house designed by Arthur Brown, G. Albert Landsburgh, and Willis Polk is distinguished by the 50-metre tower above the stage. On the entrance façade five pairs of doors give access to the vestibule, which in turn leads to the foyer, a space notable for its sculptured walls and its coffered, barrel-vaulted ceiling rising 12 metres above a marble-inlaid floor. A wide marble staircase at either end leads to the balconies. The seating capacity of the horseshoe auditorium is 3,176, distributed over the 1,300-seat orchestra stalls, a downstairs ring of boxes, and two amphitheatre balconies. The proscenium arch stretches to a width of 17.50 metres and culminates at a height of 17 metres. The sculptor Edgar Walter created the two mounted amazons ornamenting the spandrels. The electronically powered stage machinery can handle as many as 77 sets. The stage floor is divided into 29 sections, all controllable from above. The orchestra pit is large enough to accommodate an ensemble of 65 musicians.*

1979. *The backstage is extended.*
1981. *The opening of a new wing.*

In the mid-19th century San Francisco was host to many more gamblers, confidence men, and prostitutes than ballet dancers and opera singers. But the motley, gold-obsessed population rushed to mine any new vein of entertainment that might show up, even the ragtag touring opera company that opened its season in January 1851 with a performance of Bellini's *La Sonnambula*, when the soloists sang in Italian and an all-male chorus supported them in English! A year later Chinese opera had its day, unleashing all manner of unfamiliar sounds from a number of "opera-pagodas" supported by the city's large Cantonese colony. Meanwhile, a certain Tom Maguire continued to spend his saloon- and gambling-den fortune rebuilding, fire after fire, theatres in which a population accustomed to the real-life Wild West fell in love with the mock duels of operetta and bel canto. By 1876 the city was almost civilized, a boomtown where opera had become the favorite diversion of a rapidly growing middle class. One of its members, a dentist named Tom Wade, built himself a theatre in which the centerpiece of the foyer was a fountain flowing with eau de cologne. Three years later came the Tivoli Gardens, which between 1879 and 1906 gave almost 10,000 performances of grand opera, light opera, and operetta, including 41 consecutive nights of Gounod's *Faust* and 40 performances of Verdi's *Otello*. Between the onset of the Gold Rush in 1848 and the tragic earthquake of 1906, San Francisco saw no less than thirty-six theatres make their bid for the public's attention. After 1906, the city rose from its ashes and by the end of World War I San Francisco felt ready to repair the frayed links with its operatic past. The challenge would fall to Gaetano Merola, a Californian by adoption, who, in 1923, staged his first season in the Civic Auditorium, a venue with a capacity of 12,000! A decade later the city decided it was time for San Francisco to have a new opera house, a need that coincided with the desire of war veterans to commemorate their service in something other than a mausoleum. The result was the huge War Memorial Opera House, designed by Arthur Brown in a Classical-Baroque style, its monumentality matched by a stage curtain of gold brocade weighing more than a ton. The auditorium, with its capacity of more than

FACTS ABOUT THE BUILDING

1932 *Arthur Brown, G. Albert Lansburgh, and Willis Polk, architects*
Capacity: 3,176 (300 standing)
Lyre-shaped auditorium
1 orchestra stalls
1 tier of downstairs boxes
2 amphitheatre balconies
Proscenium: **width** 17.50m; **height** 17m
Stage: **width** 41m; **height** 35m; **depth** 26m

Lotte Lehmann (1888–1976).

3,000, basks in the subtle tones of a cream and brown décor illuminated by a star-burst chandelier. San Francisco's opera lovers—among the world's most passionate—enter this ambitious space through a nobly scaled foyer crowned by a coffered barrel vault; inside the auditorium they face the grandiose arch of a coffered proscenium, its spandrels supporting a pair of Art Deco amazons. In 1979 the San Francisco Opera enlarged its backstage facilities, and in 1981 it added a wing to house rehearsal studios and stages. None of this, however, could protect the War Memorial theatre from the 1989 earthquake, the effects of which are to be repaired over a period of eighteen months, beginning in 1996. When "retrofitted" and reopened, the house where so many stars have made their American debuts should be "brought down" only by vociferous applause.

Palacio de Bellas Artes
Mexico City

1905. *Construction of Adamo Boari's opera house is begun, then continued after the revolution of 1910 by the architect Antonio Muñoz and finished in 1934 by Federico E. Mariscal. The exterior measures 96 metres in length and 32 metres in height. The interior, decorated by Boari's successors, reflects the Art Deco style of the period. The frequently interrupted project was also delayed by miscalculations that caused the building to sink, a situation which persists.*

1934. *Inaugurated with performances by Viennese musicians: Karl Alwin, Franz Steiner, and William Wymetal.*

O pera in Mexico City can trace its history back to 1711 and the premiere of Manuel Zumaya's *Partenope*, the first opera written in Mexico, but it was another century before the capital possessed theatres worthy of its singers. In 1842 they had Lorenzo da la Hidalga's Santa Anna Theatre, a classical gem of a house, but a financial disaster for its impresario, who a decade later found himself obliged to rent the building and then to turn it over to the state, whereupon the Santa Anna became the National Theatre. During the reign of Maximilian, Napoleon III's puppet Emperor, the National was renamed the Imperial, only to be rechristened the National as soon as the Republic had been restored. The house came to the end of its career along with the expiring century and succumbed to the wreckers in 1901. Meanwhile, Mexico had become economically stronger, prompting the Republic's leaders to think of erecting an opera house as a symbol of national well-being. The government of Porfirio Díaz settled on the plans of an Italian architect, Adamo Boari, whose idea was to liberate classical proportion by recasting it as Art Deco and mixing in elements from pre-Hispanic America. In the end, he would out-Garnier Garnier. Boari thought big, especially when it came to the façade, which stretches almost 100 metres. To make his ambitious scheme feasible, moreover, he studied the latest technical advances of engineers in New York, particularly their use of steel-frame construction and reinforced concrete to make buildings both lighter and taller. In 1908, work got under way on the park chosen as the site of the new National Theatre. Inauguration would not come, however, for another quarter-century, during which the process unfolded like some incredible soap opera. Revolution brought construction to a halt in 1913, after which Boari managed to get it restarted, only to relinquish his place three years later to Ignacio de la Hidalga, the grandson of the architect responsible for the Santa Anna. In 1919 work stopped again, this time for ten years. In 1931 the project

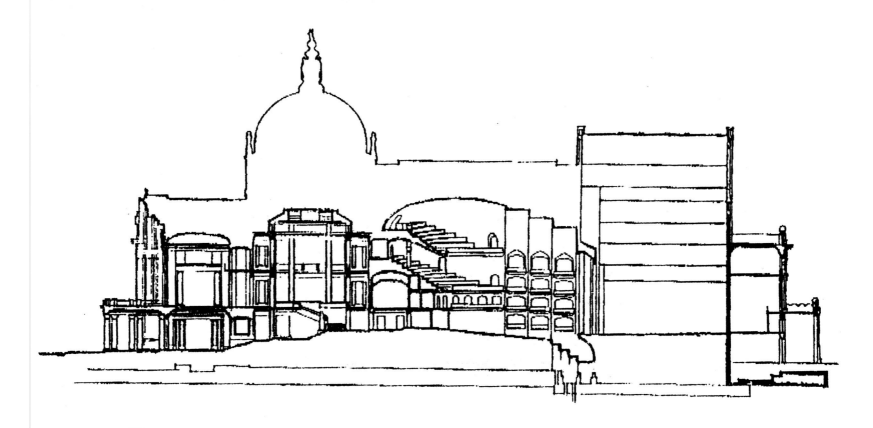

FACTS ABOUT THE THEATRE

1905 *Adam Boari followed by Antonio Muñoz and, finally, Federico E. Mariscal*
Capacity: 1,987
Horseshoe auditorium
2 balconies
Stage: **width** 12.5m; **height** 32m; **depth** 18m

was revived but then dropped anew after only a few months, convincing many that it was now totally dead. However, the Secretary of the Treasury came to the rescue, as a result of which the National Theatre emerged as the Palacio de Bellas Artes. This meant a wider mandate and thus a modification of Boari's plans, a task assigned to Federico Mariscal, who completed the building in 1934. Along the way Mexico lost the glass covering of the metal-frame dome whose crystalline flames were supposed to surge up from the Carrara-clad façade as if from a flaming pyre. Also sacrificed was the winter garden planned for the entrance hall; Boari had to make do with a pergola and even that was destroyed in 1973. On the other hand, Mariscal kept Boari's plan for the auditorium, which is almost a Bayreuth amphitheatre, except for the boxes positioned for the best possible sightlines. Also preserved is the remarkable fire curtain of galvanized iron covered with a mosaic of iridescent glass representing the Valley of Mexico. Once the opera house became a state monument, its interior decorations would be carefully maintained. The Art Deco style prevails, of course, even though from a later, more geometric stage typical of the 1930s and enriched with Aztec and Mayan motifs. Along the foyer's polychrome marble revetments, stylized jaguars and coyotes prowl among Cubist themes illuminated by Tiffany lamps. The walls decorated by some of Mexico's most important artists have not dated, a fact brought home recently when contemporary colors were used to restore the little Manuel Ponce Auditorium, where paintings and performances coexist in perfect harmony.

Glyndebourne Opera House
Sussex, England

1994. *The new theatre inaugurated on 28 May with Mozart's* The Marriage of Figaro.

The architect Michael Hopkins designed a large brick oval crowned by the auditorium's circular roof and the parallelepiped stage building with its superstructure of exposed steel. Generous glazing for windows and doors takes full advantage of the soft Sussex light and allows free circulation between the foyer and the gardens. A canopy protects the entrance. The U-shaped auditorium

In the late 1920s, John Christie, a rich man and a passionate lover of music, began organizing private performances at Glyndebourne, his family estate near Lewes on the Sussex Downs. Just as in a fairy-tale, one evening he fell in love with the soprano singing in Mozart's *The Abduction from the Seraglio*, whom he then married, even at the risk of being disinherited. Together they decided to build in 1934 a small 300-seat theatre dedicated to the rediscovery of Mozart, whose operas seemed particularly well suited to the intimate scale of the Glyndebourne Festival Opera, as the enterprise was called, using only the very best singers and conductors. Almost immediately, the experience of enjoying opera in a manorial setting, became the ultimate in cultural cachet, complete with a "Long Interval" for picnics in the park. With success, however, the theatre had to be enlarged, beginning as early as 1936, when the capacity was increased to 433 seats. By 1952, the house could accommodate an audience of nearly 600 and by 1977, 850. In the 1950s the Glyndebourne Festival Society was formed to relieve the Christie family of the financial burden the festival had become. John Christie died in 1962, but the festival continued under the leadership of his son George. In 1990 he announced plans to expand the theatre to a capacity of 1,200, the cost of which would be borne up to 90 per cent by private donors, who, in turn, would be allocated 28 per cent of the seats. Michael Hopkins won the design competition with less than unanimous approval of his project, which attempted to make modernity compatible with a Victorian country house. The stage building, especially, has been criticized for its cat's-cradle superstructure of exposed steel beams and for the lead revetment of its walls, which rise high above the conical roof over the auditorium. The exterior of the latter, with its setback and its cladding of 1.5 million bricks,

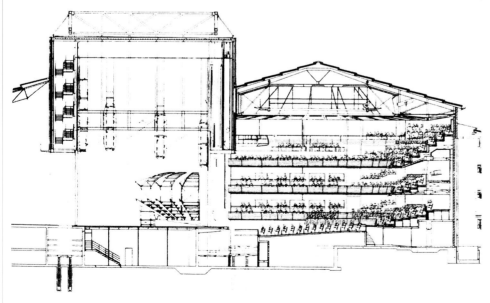

is veneered almost entirely in wood. The 1,200 seats are distributed over the orchestra stalls, two balconies, and a gallery. The stage building permits scenery to be flown, and storage is greatly facilitated by the semicircular backstage and two side stages. Much care was given to the acoustics, which were studied in a 1:50 scale model and simulated by computer at the ARUP acoustical laboratory in Cambridge.

Design for Mozart's *Magic Flute* by Simone Quaglio, 1818.

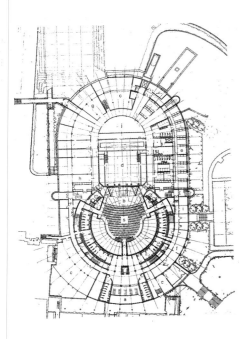

FACTS ABOUT THE BUILDING

1994 *Michael Hopkins & Partners, architects*
Capacity: 1,200
Standing room: 42
Horseshoe auditorium
1 orchestra stalls, 2 balconies, and 1 gallery
Proscenium: **width** 11.60m; **height** 9.25m
Stage: **width** 18.30m; **height** 21.34m; **depth** 17.40m

resembles the apse of an Italian Renaissance church. Inside, where warm, coppery pitch pine contrasts with charcoal-grey upholstery, the 1,200 seats are distributed throughout a horseshoe auditorium with three stairstep balconies rising above the orchestra stalls. The foyers provide views beyond the gardens towards the lake and the famous South Downs. The stage, now several metres larger than the old one, is flanked by two lateral spaces, as well as storage areas adjoining a vast rehearsal hall built into the side of a hill. Also enlarged is the orchestra pit, to a capacity of eighty musicians, and it can be raised or lowered. Sixty years after the first Glyndebourne Festival opened with *The Marriage of Figaro*, the new opera house launched its inaugural season on 28 May 1994 with the same opera. This all but guaranteed that other traditions would be respected, including the Long Interval picnic in evening dress, still closely watched by curious bovines, the only subscribers with full season tickets.

Roles reversed: the chorus watches the audience during an interval at Glyndebourne.

1934. *The Glyndebourne Festival Opera opens its first season on 28 May with Mozart's* The Marriage of Figaro, *following it on the 29th with* Così fan tutte, *both works conducted by Fritz Busch and directed by Carl Ebert. The repertory, while favoring Mozart, includes Verdi. Following World War II, it is considerably expanded to encompass such operas as Monteverdi's* L'incoronazione di Poppea, *Cavalli's* Ormindo, *Rossini's* Le Comte Ory, *Strauss's* Ariadne auf Naxos, *and Debussy's* Pelléas et Mélisande.

1946. *Kathleen Ferrier (1912-1953) makes her stage debut on 12 July, singing the title role in the world premiere of* The Rape of Lucretia *by Benjamin Britten (1913-1976). This great British singer, a rare true contralto, specialized in lieder (Schumann, Brahms, Mahler), oratorio (Bach, Handel), and "English things," but managed only two operatic roles before her untimely death at the age of forty-one. After* Lucretia, *Ferrier performed in Gluck's* Orfeo ed Euridice *(1947), again for Glyndebourne.*

World premieres at Glyndebourne include Hans Werner Henze's Elegy for Young Lovers *(1961) and Nicholas Maw's* The Rising of the Moon *(1970). Among the other 20th-century works added to the repertory are Janáček's* The Cunning Little Vixen *(1975) and* Kátya Kabanova *(1988), Prokofiev's* The Love of Three Oranges *(1982), Stravinsky's* The Rake's Progress *(1953, 1975 with designs by David Hockney), Gershwin's* Porgy and Bess *(1986), Knussen's* Where the Wild Things Are *(1984) and* Higglety, Pigglety, Pop! *(1985), Osborne's* The Electrification of the Soviet Union *(1987), and Tippett's* New Year *(1990). Under its New Opera Policy, begun in 1984, the house gives the world premiere of a new opera every two years.*

Metropolitan Opera House *New York*

1883. *The first Metropolitan Opera House, on the corner of 39th and Broadway, designed by the architect Josiah Cleaveland Cady, opens 22 October with Gounod's* Faust, *starring Christine Nilsson and Italo Campanini and conducted by Auguste Vianesi. The auditorium, dubbed the Diamond Horseshoe, is Italian style with two tiers of boxes, three balconies, and a total capacity of 3,045. At first all operas, including* Lohengrin, *are sung in Italian and then, for almost a decade, entirely in German, even* Carmen, *the opera in which Lilli Lehmann makes her Met debut.*

1892. *Fire guts the opera house, which is rebuilt within months, its capacity increased to 3,849.*

1966. *The new Metropolitan Opera House at Lincoln Center is inaugurated 16 September with the world premiere of Samuel Barber's* Antony and Cleopatra. *Production is by Franco Zeffirelli and the cast headed by Leontyne Price and Justino Diaz, under the baton of Thomas Schippers. The architecture of Wallace Harrison epitomizes 1960s modernism, albeit with a bow to tradition, as seen in the colossal, emblematic arcade and loggia across the entrance façade, the immense windows giving visual access from the outside to a pair of tall, colorful murals by Marc Chagall, the grand double*

As early as the mid-18th century operas were being performed in the outposts of the New World. By 1825 Manuel Garcia, the original Count Almaviva in Rossini's *Barbiere*, and Lorenzo Da Ponte, Mozart's librettist, could find a ready audience for Italian opera at the Park Street Theatre in New York City, giving the first American performances of *Don Giovanni* as well as a series of Rossini operas. Twenty years later Manhattan had a major opera house, the 4,600-seat Academy of Music, where every box was avidly sought by the city's rapidly expanding plutocracy. When the fabulously rich William H. Vanderbilt found it impossible to purchase one, he launched a campaign to build a grand new theatre, quickly raising $800,000 from other wealthy *refusés*—Goulds, Rockefellers, Huntingtons, Roosevelts, etc. Having found a site on the corner of Broadway and 39th Street, the underwriters proceeded with a design competition. It was won by Josiah Cleaveland Cady, who excelled in Neo-Gothic churches but could not be counted among the many, mostly European architects specializing in opera houses. With prize in hand, Cady set off for London where he inspected Covent Garden. This done, he came home and gave New York the Metropolitan, which opened in 1883, its banal exterior suggesting a cross between a bank and a grand hotel; it was sometimes likened to a brewery. However, Cady did fulfil his brief, which was to provide a large theatre in which the focus would fall on the two tiers of boxes, sufficient in number—122 in all—to satisfy the town's well-heeled socialites. So glittering was the effect on the opening night, when the Gilded Age filled every box, that the Met's auditorium became forever known as the Diamond Horseshoe. The crimson-velvet, gilt-encrusted auditorium was much larger than the even the most capacious ones in Europe. This was necessary because box-office receipts had to supply the deficiency of state subsidies. Thus, it seemed not to matter that three-quarters of the seats in the huge gallery had obstructed views, or that the backstage was little more than Seventh Avenue at the heart of the garment-manufacturing district. However, from Leopold and Walter Damrosch through Giulio Gatti-Casazza and Arturo Toscanini to Rudolph Bing and James Levine, those responsible for artistic matters at the Met have made certain that this opera house would be second to none

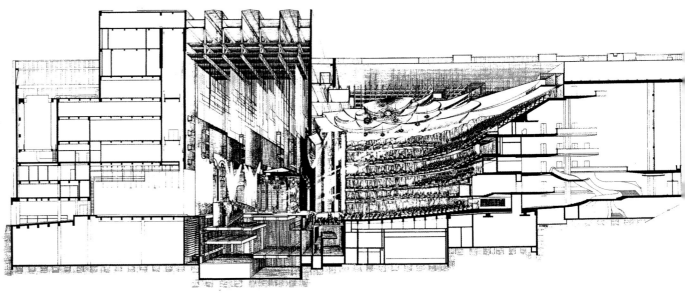

staircase in the form of a sinuous horseshoe, and the crystal chandeliers glittering like starry constellations. The chandeliers (a gift from Austria) are a theme repeated in profusion throughout the vast auditorium, where they hang from the ceiling both as a large central burst and as a diadem of smaller fires that slowly rise before and then drop after every performance, becoming an applause-getting spectacle in their own right. The stage, together with its rear and side stages, its turntable, elevators, and computerized machinery, its numerous dressing rooms and rehearsal halls, is the largest and most technologically advanced of any opera house in the world.

in the vocal power and glory of its casts. With the economic boom of the postwar years came a tremendous cultural boom throughout the United States. The old Met was considered passé. Among the numerous museums and theatres that arose at this time, the most spectacular was New York City's Lincoln Center of the Performing Arts. Here, the centerpiece became the new Metropolitan Opera House, opened in September 1966 and surrounded by the New York State Theatre (the home of the New York City Opera and Ballet), the Philharmonic Hall, the Vivian Beaumont Theatre, and the Julliard School of Music, all disposed with classical symmetry about a plaza inspired by the Campidoglio in Rome. Thanks in part to its long, continuous season (seven performances a week), its large repertory system, its regular program of new productions, its radio and television broadcasts, its complete recordings and efficient management, the Met continues today, just as in Caruso's time, to attract and hold the very greatest singers. Caruso appeared 628 times on the stage of the old house, and by 1993-1994, when both Placido Domingo and Luciano Pavarotti celebrated their 25th season in the new house, the two supertenors had performed more frequently there than on any other stage. Meanwhile, James Levine has built the orchestra into a world-class ensemble, equal to the New York Philharmonic next door.

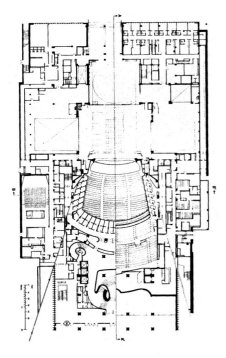

FACTS ABOUT THE BUILDINGS

1882 *Josiah Cleaveland Cady, architect, Old Metropolitan Opera House*
1965-1966 *Wallace Harrison, architect, New Metropolitan Opera House at the Lincoln Center*

Horseshoe auditorium
Capacity: 3,824 (253 standing)
1 tier of boxes
4 tiers of side boxes
4 balconies
Proscenium: **width** 17.50m, **height** 17.50m
Stage: **width** 32.70m, **height** 35.65m, **depth** 25.90m

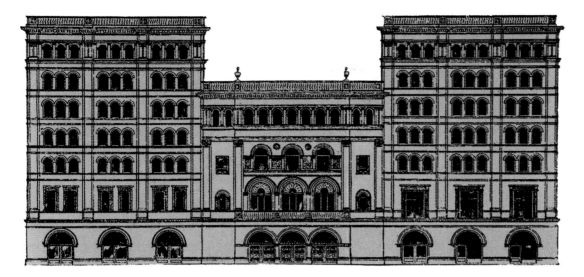

1883-1908. *Under the regimes of Henry Abbey, Leopold Damrosch, Maurice Grau, and Heinrich Conried, the Met audience enjoys regular performances by a whole galaxy of Golden Age stars. The operas of Richard Wagner are given often, including* Parsifal, *which has its first staged performance (unauthorized) outside Bayreuth in the 1903-1904 season. The American premiere of Strauss's* Salome *(1907), starring Fremstad, so shocks New York that the Met would not reschedule it until 1933.*

1908-1935. *During these years General Manager Giulio Gatti-Casazza assures the Met the greatest roster of singers in the world: Caruso, Farrar, and Fremstad, Lucrezia Bori, Emmy Destinn, Amelita Galli-Curci, Maria Jeritza, Lotte Lehmann, Claudia Muzio, Lily Pons, Rosa Ponselle, Elisabeth Rethberg, Louisa Tetrazzini, Beniamino Gigli, Giuseppe De Luca, Edward Johnson, Giovanni Martinelli, Lauritz Melchior, Tito Schipa, Antonio Scotti, Georges Thill, and the Americans Grace Moore and Lawrence Tibbett. Their most important conductors are Arturo Toscanini, Gustav Mahler, and Artur Bodanzky. At the last minute in 1934-1935, following a cancellation, the Met engages a largely unknown Norwegian singer named Kirsten Flagstad and launches one of the most remarkable of all Wagnerian careers.*

1935-1950. *Edward Johnson, a Canadian tenor with a distinguished career in Europe as well as at the Met, succeeds Gatti-Casazza as General Manager. During World War II, the Met becomes a haven not only for European singers but also for conductors: Beecham, Walter, Reiner, Leinsdorf, and Szell. Johnson introduces Jussi Bjoerling, Zinka Milanov, Jarmila Novotná, Bidù Sayão, Kerstin Thorborg, and Ljuba Welitsch. He also opens the door wide to American singers: Margaret Harshaw, Dorothy Kirsten, Regina Resnik, Eleanor Steber, Risë Stevens, Helen Traubel, Blanche Thebom, Jerome Hines, Robert Merrill, Jan Peerce, Richard Tucker, and Leonard Warren.*

1950-1972. *Rudolph Bing, after a career at the Glyndebourne and Edinburgh Festivals, becomes the most powerful General Manager since Gatti-Casazza. He introduces the era of star directors, among them Margaret Webster, Garsin Kanin, Peter Brook, Tyrone Guthrie, Alfred Lunt, Franco Zeffirelli, Nathaniel Merrill, Otto Schenk, and Jean-Louis Barrault. He has as well a sure instinct for extraordinary singers. Virtually every great operatic star enjoyed outstanding success in productions at the Met. Bing's roster of conductors includes Claudio Abbado, Ernest Ansermet, Leonard Bernstein, Karl Böhm, Colin Davis, Josef Krips, Lorin Maazel, Zubin Mehta, Dimitri Metropoulos, Thomas Schippers, Georg Solti, Leopold Stokowski, Christoph von Dohnányi, Herbert von Karajan, and James Levine.*

1971–present. *The James Levine era, when the Met prospers as never before, with many of the artists recruited by Rudolph Bing, but also with a fresh emphasis on artistic matters. Among these is the quality of the huge orchestra, which has now attained a status equal to that of the New York Philharmonic. The Met orchestra even performs, tours, and records as a regular symphonic ensemble with a repertory beyond the operatic canon.*

Premieres at the Met. *The Met—whose repertory runs deep in Bellini, Donizetti, Puccini, Verdi, Wagner, Mozart, and Richard Strauss, with periodic forays into Debussy, Massenet, Gounod, Giordano, Moussorgsky, Tchaikovsky, Berg, and Janácek—has staged scores of US premieres but relatively few world premieres, some of them nonetheless quite notable: Puccini's* La Fanciulla del West *(1910) and* Il Trittico *(1918), Humperdinck's* Die Königskinder *(1910), Giordano's* Madame Sans-Gêne *(1915), Granados's* Goyescas *(1916), Taylor's* The King's Henchman *(1927) and* Peter Ibbetson *(1931), Barber's* Vanessa *(1958) and* Antony and Cleopatra *(1966), Corigliano's* The Ghosts of Versailles *(1991), and Glass's* The Voyage *(1992).*

Maria Callas (1923–1977).

Theater for the
Performing Arts
New Orleans

The cultural heritage of New Orleans is mixed—French, then Spanish, then French again. In 1803 Napoleon sold the whole of the vast Louisiana Territory to the United States. New Orleans's Creole culture, however, did not immediately buy into American ways, and it remains a distinctive, colorful presence almost two centuries later. As early as 1792 the city had the Théâtre Saint-Pierre which in 1796 staged Grétry's *Sylvain*, the first opera known to have been performed in New Orleans. Next came the Théâtre Saint-Philippe, which opened in 1808 with Méhul's *Une Folie* before moving on to Dalayrac and Boieldieu. With each new success, French opera gained a stronger foothold in the New World, confirmed in 1815 by the erection of the Théâtre d'Orléans in the Vieux Carré, only a year before fire left it a heap of ashes. The house would be reconstructed in 1819, thanks to John Davis, a Parisian impresario and astute businessman who oversaw the decorations, created screened boxes for families still in mourning, introduced Italian opera, and enhanced revenues by constructing a hotel and dance hall next door. The Théâtre d'Orléans remained the city's principal opera house for the next forty years, but by 1824 Davis had a rival in the person of James H. Caldwell, who built the Camp Street Theatre and, in 1835, the lavish St. Charles Theatre, where he staged the United States premieres of operas by Rossini, Bellini, and Donizetti. With a capacity of 4,100, the St. Charles was the largest theatre in the Western hemisphere, a venue up to the challenge of French grand opera on the scale of Meyerbeer, whose work Caldwell presented as part of his ongoing competition with Davis. In 1842 fire struck again, this time destroying the St. Charles, which saved its rival, the Théâtre d'Orléans, but only until 1845, when a balcony collapsed, killing a good number of people. In December 1859 Charles Boudousquié opened the 1,800-seat French Opera House on Bourbon Street with Rossini's *William Tell*. The finest theatre in the United States at the time, the French Opera House engaged for its second season the seventeen-year-old Adelina Patti, who undertook seven roles in three months: Lucia, Gilda, Rosina, Valentine, Dinorah, Lady Harriet, and the *Trovatore* Leonora! Soon the Civil War would radically reduce activities at the French Opera House, which survived only to lose its singers and musicians when their ship went down at sea

in 1866. By the 1870s, however, opera was flourishing in New Orleans, where, before the end of the 19th century, some 170 operas received their United States premieres, more than in any American city except New York. After the turn of the century, however, decline set in, forcing the theatre to cease operations in 1913. New Orleans was now less interested in bel canto than in blues and jazz, both of which it had spawned. Still, following restoration to repair storm damage, the French Opera House reopened on 11 November, a mere two weeks before fire wrought its usual havoc. Not until 1943 would New Orleans again have its own opera troupe, which, alas, had to perform in the City Park or the Municipal Auditorium, neither of them blessed with ideal acoustics or a decent orchestra pit. Thirty years later, in 1973, things improved radically, thanks to the New Orleans Theatre for the Performing Arts, a 2,317-seat venue that has brought new operatic lustre to the banks of the Mississippi.

FACTS ABOUT THE BUILDING

1973 *Edward Mathes of Mathes, Bergman & Associates and Henry Banker & Associates, architects*
Capacity: 2,317
Fan-shaped auditorium
1 balcony
Proscenium: **width** 19.44m; **height** 10.37m
Stage: **width** 51.84m; **height** 29.16m; **depth** 24.30m

Musiektheater
Amsterdam

MUSIEKTHEATER
*Amsterdam - The
Netherlands*

1986. *Inaugurated 23 September with
the world premiere of* Ithaka, *an
English-language opera by the Dutch
composer Otto Ketting with a libretto
by the composer and Kees Hin. A few
days later the season began with Verdi's*
Falstaff.

*The total cost of the new opera house
designed by the Dutch architect Cees
Dam in collaboration with Wilhelm
Holzbauer came to 400 million francs.
Over 3,000 pilings serve to anchor the
building to the marshy soil of its river-
side location. The curving red-brick
façade is girdled with 6 portals pierced
by huge square-mullioned windows.*

In 1986, the municipality of Amsterdam decided to move its offices to a former industrial site along the River Amstel, a change contemplated since 1954. A new opera house had been in urgent discussion since the early 1980s, and the city officials were prompted to combine the two projects within the same structure and thus create a kind of red-brick citadel—a civic and cultural center—designed by Cees Dam and Wilhelm Holzbauer. To keep opera lovers from getting lost in the herd of ordinary citizens, the entrance to the theatre would be set apart by six giant white-stone portals opening wide to the exterior but hugging the curved shaped of the auditorium within. The hall is a segment of a circle with two balconies, the first of which projects slightly at the center to form a kind of royal box, the whole evoking the classicism of Ledoux in Besançon and Soufflot in Lyons. On the stage, Amsterdam demonstrated its grasp of musical theatre by engineering a stage capable of moving forward to cover the orchestra pit all the way to the first row of seats. As for productions, they are designed to be both efficient and economical. Left of the main stage is a second or lateral stage, while dressing rooms on the right put performers close to the stage. Backstage a scenery workshop produces sets that roll on stage as complete units, and a single control panel operates the turntable. Thus, everything combines to permit the kind of rapid scene change required by a repertory with a bias towards contemporary works.

FACTS ABOUT THE BUILDING

1986 *Cees Dam and Wilhelm Holzhauer,
architects*
Capacity: 1,600
Fan-shaped auditorium
1 orchestra stalls amphitheatre style
2 amphitheatre balconies
Stage: width 14-21m; height 10m; depth 20-
35m

The Cairo Opera House

THE CAIRO OPERA HOUSE
Cairo - Egypt

1869. *Khedive Ismaïl Pasha commissions Italian architects Avoscani and Rossi to design and construct an 850-seat opera house, which is inaugurated on 1 November with Verdi's* Rigoletto.

1971. *A fire completely destroys the theatre on the night of 28 October.*

1983. *In April the Japanese government informs President Hosni Mubarak of its desire to make the Egyptian people a gift of $30 million for an opera house.*

1984. *The Japanese architect Kuashiro Shikeda begins work on 20 March. The project takes 34 months to complete.*

1988. *Inaugurated 10 October with a program of Egyptian music and Kabuki. The courtyards, domes, and arches are clad in beige stone. White Italian marble and Belgian stained glass form part of a perfectly integrated complex on the west bank of the Nile.*

FACTS ABOUT THE BUILDING

1869 *Avoscani and Rossi, architects*
1988 *Kuashiro Shikeda, architect*
Capacity: 1,200 (main auditorium); 450 (small theatre)
Amphitheatre plan
1 orchestra stalls, 3 tiers of boxes, 1 top gallery
Proscenium: **width** 16m; **height** 9m
Stage: **width** 20m; **height** 28m; **depth** 19m

Contrary to long-held popular belief, it was not the trumpet fanfares of Verdi's *Aida* that inaugurated the Cairo Opera House in 1869 but the curses of *Rigoletto*. Earlier that year the Khedive Ismaïl Pasha had decided to celebrate the opening of the Suez Canal by replacing the old vice-regal theatre with a new building. It took only six months to erect the house, from plans by two Italian architects, Avoscani and Rossi, who designed an 850-seat auditorium composed of orchestra stalls, three tiers of boxes, and a top gallery. The acoustics proved so remarkable that twenty years later an attempt would be made to duplicate them at Bastia in far-off Corsica. The Khedive reserved for himself not merely the official box but also an additional pair of enclosed boxes for his harem. For the first performance he invited every crowned head in Europe. Verdi was asked to write a new opera, but he was disinclined to compose a *pièce d'occasion*, and instead offered *Rigoletto*, then almost twenty years old. Cairo would not see *Aida* for another two years, following a gestation that might have been the basis of an opera itself. The story was by the French Egyptologist Auguste Mariette; Verdi demanded a fee worthy of a pharaoh and the sets were marooned in Paris by the Franco-Prussian War of 1870. But in the end it was a triumphant premiere, and the Italian delegate was made a Commander of the Ottoman Empire. Soon thereafter, alas, the Cairo Opera went into decline and finally into bankruptcy in 1877, followed in 1879 by the fall of Ismaïl Pasha himself. The Opera House was managed by a succession of impresarios until the Italians took over. Finally, on the night of 28 October 1971 a short circuit sparked a raging fire that finished off the theatre. The site cleared, it became a parking lot. Lack of funds meant that all plans to rebuild remained on the shelf until 1983, when President Hosni Mubarak made a state visit to Japan, which offered to contribute $30 million towards the construction of a new opera house for Cairo. The Japanese even provided a major architect, Kuashiro Shikeda, who designed a modern Islamic complex on the banks of the Nile halfway between the old quarters and the new residential quarter near Cairo University. The floors are paved with white Italian marble and the windows filled with stained glass from Belgium. Beneath a cluster of domes, crenellated courtyards, and arches, all clad in

1871. *World premiere of Verdi's Aida on 25 December.*

It would take Cecil B. De Mille to do justice to the story of how Aida *came into being. From a plot suggested by the French Egyptologist Auguste Mariette, Camille du Locle, director of the Opéra-Comique in Paris, prepared a book in French, which then became the basis for the Italian libretto by Antonio Ghislanzoni. First, the scenario had to be submitted to the Khedive of Egypt, who, pleased, offered it to Verdi. The composer, though excited by the project, insisted upon retaining strict control of the libretto and the choice of a conductor. He also demanded a fee of 150,000 gold francs (four times more than for* Don Carlos*) and insisted upon an Italian text, whereas Mariette had envisioned a French text for francophone Cairo. Ghislanzoni thus had to work from the scenario prepared by the French archaeologist, who would never be paid for his contribution. By January 1870 the opera was ready, just in time for the Franco-Prussian War to keep the sets and costumes from leaving Paris. As a result, the premiere had to be put off until 24 December 1871. Hardly had the curtain rung down when Verdi received a telegram announcing a* succès *splendissime. The patriotic Italian composer now found himself named honorary Commander of the Ottoman Empire. After* Aida *received its triumphant premiere at La Scala on 8 February 1872, Verdi took 32 curtain calls. Later he commented: "It's probably not the worst thing I've written. The audience seems to have liked it. I think it will sell out almost any house. . . ." Even today,* Aida *remains the most popular opera in Egypt, where, since 1912, it is performed every year at the foot of the pyramids.*

Set for Act II of Verdi's *Aida* by J.B. Lavastre.

ochre stone matching that of the ancient pyramids, are a 1,200-seat auditorium, a second, 450-seat hall, and an open-air theatre with an audience capacity of 1,000. After almost three years of work, overseen by Japanese engineers, the new Cairo Opera House opened on 10 October 1988, once again without *Aida*, but with a mixed program of Egyptian music and Kabuki—an expression of gratitude to the maecenas from the Far East.

Arts Center
Seoul, Korea

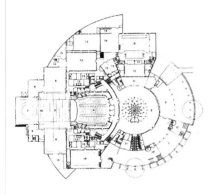
In operatic matters (as in so many others) Korea has very quickly made up for whatever it lacked in the past. In 1910 a nation that had escaped colonialism suddenly found itself annexed by Japan, whose arsenal of conquest did not include Western music. Only after the Korean War (1950-1953), which confirmed the peninsula's division along the 38th parallel, did South Korea begin to discover opera, spurred on by the establishment of North Korea's National Opera in the late 1950s. Now the Seoul regime began organizing its own company, which fearlessly took on the Italian repertory in vernacular translation, staging performances before audiences of 4,000 packed into Citizens' Hall. By 1973 Seoul had built a new complex on the outskirts of the city which included an auditorium whose 1,500 capacity proved more comfortable for Korean voices. However, the country reverted to type in 1979 when a new 4,000-seat barn was erected within the Sejong Cultural Center. Finally, at the end of the 1980s, the economic flowering of South Korea made it possible for the capital to begin work on the Seoul Arts Center. Opened in 1992, the Center is so well endowed as to have its own underground communications system. The opera house, designed by Seok Chul Kim, coils up inside a gigantic conch shell, an organic form dictated by the building's various functions. At the center of the spiral is a vast rotunda giving access to the first ring and thus to the opera house proper, with its 2,400 seats, as well as to the 700-seat theatre and an adaptable hall. The scenery workshops, the backstage areas, the spaces for prop storage and rehearsals, all cling to the shell's exterior and its carapace of glass and marble slabs. With its 'snail theatre' Seoul could be said to have squared the circle, but there is nothing new under the sun, as every wise person knows; thus, a longitudinal section of this futuristic monument would reveal something very similar to great lyric theatres of the 19th century.

Suomen Kansallisooppera
Helsinki

1994. *Inaugurated 30 November with, first, an excerpt from Pacius's* The Hunt of King Charles, *followed by the "Gloria" from Beethoven's* Missa Solemnis *and the whole of Aulis Sallinen's* Kullervo, *the latter directed by Kalle Holmberg and sung by Jorma Hynninen and Eeva-Liisa Saarinen.*

Several days later Bizet's Carmen *inaugurated the new stage with a full-length opera, eighty-two years after it had first been performed in Helsinki, under the baton of Merikanto.*
On 4 December a gala evening brought together Tom Krause, Matti Salminen, and Karita Mattila, who performed excerpts from Tannhäuser, La Favorita, Tosca, *and* The Hunt of King Charles.
The Suomen Kansallisooppera is now host to an annual May opera festival.

FACTS ABOUT THE BUILDING

1981 *Eero Hyvämäki, Jukka Karhunen, and Risto Parkkinen, architects*
1 main, 1,385-seat horseshoe auditorium with 3 balconies
1 small, 200-500 adaptable hall
Proscenium: **width** 17m, **height** 10m
Stage: **width** 18m, **height** 12.80m, **depth** 12m

When opera came to Helsinki in 1879 it found a home at the 500-seat Alexander Theatre, a garrison facility built by the occupying Russians. For a long time thereafter the city had to make do with this little French-style auditorium built like a miniature version of the Maryinsky in St. Petersburg. Then came independence from Russia in 1917, which allowed Finland, as early as 1919, to select Toolo Bay as the site for a new opera house. In 1964, Alvar Aalto, the great Finnish modernist, suggested that the building be erected along the water's edge, where he was already involved in constructing the Finlandia Theatre. Only in 1975, however, did the municipality embrace the idea and announce a nation-wide design competition. Eero Hyvämäki, Jukka Karhunen, and Risto Parkkinen won the prize jointly and submitted their plans in 1981. It then took another twelve years to complete the complex, in all its 40,000 square metres, a play of intersecting grids, blind on the stage side and open on the bay, where foyers overlook the water through a large, square-mullioned window in the spirit of the Bauhaus. Geometric and functional, the building reveals nothing of its true nature except where the cubic mass gives way to curves signifying the front of the stage building or the shell of the auditorium. The complex seems almost clinically cold until one has got beyond the vestibule. The immense foyer, moreover, still retains a touch of the exhibition hall it originally was. As for the auditorium, it is the beneficiary of the most advanced acoustical research, research that persuaded the architects to choose a horseshoe plan with three projecting balconies which recede like an amphitheatre rather than overhanging the orchestra stalls. Functionalism dominates the stage, whose plan is similar to one drawn up about the same time for the Opéra de la Bastille in Paris. Although entirely rational, Helsinki's opera house faced serious objections from part of the Finnish population, causing a delay that forced Aulis Sallinen to grant Los Angeles, rather than Helsinki, the premiere of a work he had written to celebrate both the opening of the Suomen Kansallisooppera and the seventy-fifth anniversary of Finland's independence.

VI Theatres of
the Future

Festspielhaus Bayreuth

1876. *Inaugurated with the first complete* Ring *Cycle* (Der Ring des Niebelungen)—Das Rheingold, Die Walküre, Siegfried, *and* Götterdämmerung—*conducted by Hans Richter. In the audience are Liszt, Grieg, Bruckner, Mahler, Tchaikovsky, Saint-Saëns, Nietzsche, Tolstoy, Kaiser Wilhelm I, and Ludwig II of Bavaria.*

Wagner had to wait more than a quarter of a century before he could see his immense dream come true. The dream began with a project for a simple, wood theatre in a field near Zurich where he and the architect Gottfried von Semper planned to stage *The Death of Siegfried* and then, after three performances, burn both the building and the score. The final realization came in 1876 when Wagner's own Festspielhaus opened in Bayreuth with the first complete performance of *Der Ring des Niebelungen*, all four mighty operas conducted by Hans Richter. In his preface to the first edition of the *Ring* libretto (1862), the composer had established the key aspects of the future theatre, with its orchestra pit out of sight and its auditorium like the semicircular end of a stadium, long and steeply raked. To many, all this signified pure Utopia, but Wagner and Semper fully intended to erect a temporary theatre on these lines inside Munich's Glast Palast. It was not to be, however, owing to intrigues at the court of King Ludwig II of Bavaria, his protector. Once again Wagner had to put the theatre on hold, which released Semper to leave for Dresden, where he quickly forgot their shared theories while turning to a monumental project of his own. Not until 1871 did the composer discover the ideal site, a hilltop overlooking Bayreuth, which he chose for its pastoral tranquillity. Back in Munich, King Ludwig once again had to rescue Wagner, following the defection of too many subscribers, and thus allow construction to begin, under the supervision

1748. *The Baroque theatre of Bayreuth designed by Giuseppe Galli-Bibiena for the Margravine Wilhelmina of Prussia is inaugurated with Hasse's* Ezio.
1864. *King Ludwig II commissions Wagner to build a theatre to his own specifications.*
1872. *The building's cornerstone is laid, accompanied by Beethoven's Ninth Symphony under the baton of Wagner himself. True to his theories, Wagner combined music, poetry, drama, dance, and the visual arts in a unified art work, a* Gesamtkunstwerk. *Lacking expertise in architecture, Wagner assures the success of his revolutionary enterprise by engaging the cooperation of the architect Otto Brückwald and the Bavarian court engineer Karl Brandt. According to Wagner: "There is no architecture in the world that can make beauty out of superimposing and . . . dividing an audience into classes and castes of citizens. . . ." Thus, Bayreuth has no balconies or galleries but only orchestra stalls in curved rows so that every member of the audience can see and hear equally well. Even so, Ludwig II insisted upon boxes for the nobility, tucked in along the rear wall behind a colonnade of square piers, above which is another narrow row of boxes for the attendants. The musicians are placed under the stage in six rows that slant away from the audience at the same angle as the orchestra stalls, their position partially covered by the lip of the stage. This endows the sound of the 130-member orchestra with a mysterious, distant quality and keeps it from overwhelming the singers. The effect, together with the double proscenium and the diminishing series of right-angle wall sections on either side of the auditorium (a contribution of Karl Brandt), creates that "mystic gulf" (*mystischer Abgrund*) that Wagner wanted so much to exist between performers and audience. In the years 1962-1974 the old-fashioned half-timbering gave way to cement, the stage had its wooden structural frame replaced with steel, its machinery brought up to date, and prop storage added to the back.*

Wagner conducting Beethoven's Ninth Symphony, May 22nd, 1872, in the old Opera House of Bayreuth to celebrate laying the foundation stone of the Festspielhaus.

of the court architect, Otto Brückwald, and the engineer Karl Brandt. It was the latter who created the famous "mystic gulf," the orchestra pit hidden from the audience by a pair of hoods and raked downward under the stage. The auditorium consists of a single wedge-shaped block of seats, expanding in width towards the back and framed by sections of wall projecting at right angles, with columns and entablature like those forming the proscenium, decreasing in projection as they recede from the stage. These features may look odd but they contribute to the exceptional acoustics of a hall in which nothing is allowed to distract the viewer's eye, not even light. For the first time in any theatre the lights were lowered during performance. At the King's request, boxes were fitted into the rear wall behind a Palladian colonnade, which also enhanced the beautiful sound. For the arrival of Ludwig II at the premiere of *Parsifal* in 1882, a balcony was added above the entrance, which ruptured the spartan unity of the half-timbered brick façade. Wagner wanted no embellishments on a theatre he regarded as an experiment, planning to replace it eventually with a building more in keeping with the opulent taste of the late 19th century. For lack of subsidies, the provisional became the definitive, except on the stage where, beginning in 1960, the obsolete machinery would be replaced. A theatre for the future even today, thanks to its productions, the Bayreuth Festspielhaus is nonetheless linked to the past by virtue of its dedication to one body of work, a privilege jealously guarded by the composer's heirs.

Gwyneth Jones as Brünnhilde in Wagner's *Ring*, produced by Patrice Chéreau to celebrate the hundredth anniversary of the Bayreuth Festival, 1976.

FACTS ABOUT THE BUILDING

1876 *Richard Wagner, Otto Brückwald, and Karl Brandt, architects*
1962-1974 *Work designed to modernize the house and secure it against fire.*
Capacity: 1,925
Proscenium: **width** 13m, **height** 12m
Stage: **width** 27m, **height** 26m, **depth** 22m

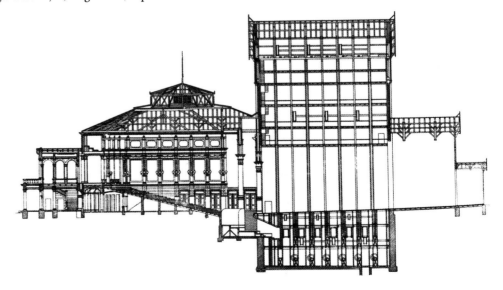

1976. *To mark the centenary of the Festspielhaus, Wolfgang Wagner, the director of the Bayreuth Festival, recruited Patrice Chéreau, Pierre Boulez, Richard Peduzzi, and Jacques Schmidt (the latter for the television film) to take a whole new approach to the* Ring. *This post-modern "French" cycle proved controversial but also, by most accounts, unforgettably effective. The production ran until 1979. Pierre Boulez tells of the opposition he faced as the conductor of an orchestra composed largely of musicians from other German theatres and groups who were giving their month's annual holiday to play at Bayreuth. The running time for each of the four operas would be very close to that of performances given under Hans Richter in 1876. Chéreau and Peduzzi threw themselves into the problems of design and came up with some extraordinary, even surreal solutions. Chéreau wanted sets conjuring a poetic vision, "even if water must be water, the trees real trees, and the giants actual giants." The complete* Ring *produced in 1976 cost—sets, costumes, special effects, and labor included—roughly $350,000 or £225,000.*

Richard Wagner by Peter Maynard, after a photograph by Petit and Tronquart. Private collection.

To achieve such powerful effects for so little money meant using plastic rather than metal for the Valkyries' breast plates, borrowing shoes from other productions, other props from Parsifal *and a pair of big metal doors from the Théâtre National Populaire in Villeurbanne.*

Santa Fe Opera
New Mexico

1957. *Inaugurated 3 July, launching a season ambitious enough to include* The Rake's Progress, *produced under the supervision of Stravinsky himself.*
1957-1995. *Among the 113 operas staged in the big theatre under the Western sky are 35 premieres, including Levy's* The Tower *(1957), Floyd's* Wuthering Heights *(1958), Berio's* Opera *(1970), Villa-Lobos's* Yerma *(1971), and Lang's* Modern Painters *(1995). The annual season begins at the end of June.*
Richard Strauss. *The Santa Fe Opera has specialized in the works of Richard Strauss, presenting every opera in the composer's canon except* Die Frau ohne Schatten *and* Guntram. *Die ägyptische Helena, Capriccio, Daphne, Friedenstag, Intermezzo, and* Die Liebe der Danae *all received their first fully staged, professional performances in the United States at the Santa Fe Opera.*

FACTS ABOUT THE BUILDING

1967 McHugh and Kidder, architects
1995-1997 James Stewart Polshek and Partners, architects of the expansion
Capacity: 1,889 (eventually 2,168)
1 amphitheatre orchestra stalls
1 amphitheatre balcony
Stage: **width** 18.15m; **height** 5.20m; **depth** 21m

One day in the middle of this century the parents of a boy called John Crosby, who suffered from asthma, sent him to Santa Fe, to live under the sun in the high, dry air of New Mexico. Years later the adult John Crosby, watching Fritz Reiner conduct at New York's Metropolitan Opera, caught another bug, the opera virus. Combining the practical with the pleasurable, Crosby founded the Santa Fe Opera in July 1957 in the foothills of the Sangre de Cristo Mountains, where, in a natural bowl, he erected a simple alfresco venue with 480 seats, the star-spangled heavens for a vault, and a company of 67, without stars. Armed with light wool blankets, the mostly neophyte audience discovered the standard repertory, of course, but also the late operas of Richard Strauss, works long disdained in the United States, or brand new works, which the opinionated Crosby persisted in scheduling year after year. Indeed, it was following the American premiere of Hindemith's *Cardillac* in 1967 that fire swept through and destroyed the wood-built theatre which had slowly grown along with its audience. By the following summer, however, a new auditorium had been built in the shape of a cone from which the sound emerges, but open at the sides. The partially covered auditorium can accommodate almost 1,900 spectators, while the hood covering the stage and backstage shelters a company numbering up to 600 persons. A fresh campaign is now under way to increase the audience capacity by 279. When complete, the expanded roofs over the auditorium and stage will be connected by an immense transparent membrane of glass—offering protection for every seat while still giving visual access to the world's most sublime sky.

Opera House
Sydney

OPERA HOUSE
Sydney - Australia

1955. *The New South Wales government opens a design competition for the Sydney Opera House.*
1957. *Jørn Utzon, a pupil of Alvar Aalto, wins the competition over 233 other aspirants.*
1966. *Buffeted by political and financial storms, Utzon abandons his project, to be replaced by E.H. Farmer, Peter Hall, Lionel Todd, and David Littlemore.*
1973. *Finished 20 October, the complex includes restaurants, promenades, and foyers, all in the service of a big concert hall, an opera theatre, a drama theatre, and a cinema. During construction it became apparent that the largest hall could be used only for concerts, which left the 1,500-seat venue to become the opera house. Benjamin Britten, when asked whether this would be sufficient, replied yes, as long as the musicians are Japanese and play only piccolos. In reality, the Opera Theatre is a technological jewel incorporating a complex lighting system, a revolving stage with two built-in platforms, below-stage set storage, and four 40-foot square lifts for vertical handling of scenery. The orchestra pit holds a maximum of 75 musicians. The acoustical engineer was the Dane Wilhelm Lassen. It was inaugurated 28 September with Prokofiev's* War and Peace.

S ome see a majestic windjammer sailing into the harbor, others a pair of giant turtles in the mating season, but whatever the impression, there can be no doubt about the engineering miracle represented by the Sydney Opera House. Even more miraculous, however, is the fact that Australia finally succeeded in creating an opera company. For more than a century opera in Australia had been a matter of touring companies, until the early 1950s when a national troupe emerged, thus raising the issue of a suitably equipped home. In 1955 the New South Wales government announced an international design competition. It was won by a young and unknown Danish architect named Jørn Utzon. From that moment a succession of storms would roll across Sydney Harbor for years to come. To begin with, Utzon's project, seductive as it looked, was unsupported by any serious study; it posed such nightmarish engineering problems (brilliantly solved by the firm of Ove Arup) that costs, despite constant review, rose to three and a half times the original budget, causing a political backlash against a design that already had its opponents. The cornerstone was laid in 1959, but it would take five years of calculation before the gigantic "sails" of tile-clad concrete attained their full height, some 60 metres above the ground. By 1965 the shell had been finished, generating great public interest, but it was an empty shell. While Utzon busied himself with designing china for the restaurants, the political storm grew ever

more violent until finally the architect resigned and abandoned the project, a victim of party quarrels. When it was inaugurated he refused to attend. The government then commissioned four Australian architects to finish the complex, a process that required another seven years. The first battle they faced was a reconfiguring of the interior so as to create five halls

The Sydney Opera House, erected on Bennelong Point in Sydney Harbor, is opera's ultramodern emblem. Opera found a place in Australian life way back in the 19th century, succeeding well enough to nurture the young talents of the Australian soprano **Nellie Melba** (1861-1931). Born in Melbourne, this great star of opera's Golden Age made her debut as a singer at Melbourne Town Hall in March 1884. After studies in Paris with the celebrated teacher Mathilde Marchesi, she made her first operatic appearance in Europe at La Monnaie in Brussels, where she won tremendous acclaim for her performance as Gilda in Verdi's Rigoletto. Thereafter Melba (opposite) sang all over the world, with particular success at London's Covent Garden, where she long reigned as prima donna assoluta. It was not until 1911, however, that Melba made her first triumphant tour of Australia.

Joan Sutherland (1926—), born in Sydney, began her climb to international operatic fame in 1949 when she won a local competition, the proceeds from which enabled to her resign from her secretarial job and study full time. Soon thereafter she was in London, for further study and a debut in 1952 at Covent Garden, where she began in small roles, such as the First Lady in The Magic Flute and Clothilde in Norma, the latter with Maria Callas in the title role. Meanwhile, Sutherland married Richard Bonynge, a fellow Australian who became her vocal coach, accompanist, and finally conductor. Encouraged by Bonynge, Sutherland discovered her soaring upper register, her gift for coloratura, and the bel canto repertory. With her Covent Garden debut in 1959 in Donizetti's Lucia di Lammermoor, directed by Franco Zeffirelli, Sutherland was well launched into one of the century's most brilliant careers, which ended only with her retirement in 1990. In 1965 she and Bonynge returned to Australia for a tumultuously successful tour at the head of their own operatic company.

Richard Bonynge (1930—), born in Epping, New South Wales, made his

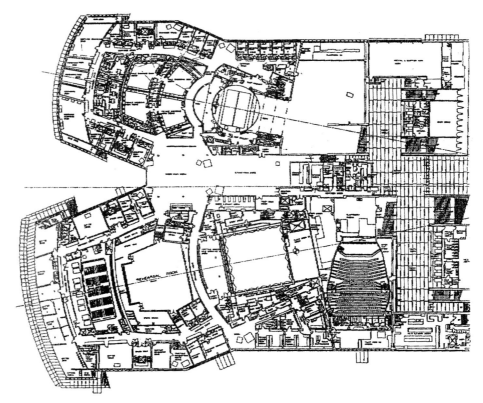

instead of three, convert the 2,800-seat opera auditorium into a concert hall, and transfer the opera to the smaller, 1,500-seat theatre with a revolving stage but no backstage area or flies. What an irony that a theatre meant to dazzle the world, a theatre whose silhouette has become the very emblem of Sydney, an overall complex with a total audience capacity of 5,500, some 1,000 different rooms, and entrance halls like cathedral naves—this Australian miracle ends up not even fulfilling its primary function, that of an opera house a cut above an ordinary, all-purpose auditorium.

Nellie Melba (1861-1931)

conductorial debut in 1963 at the Vancouver International Festival, where he conducted performances of Gounod's Faust *in which his wife, Joan Sutherland, sang Marguerite. The following year he was on the podium at Covent Garden for performances of Bellini's* I Puritani, *again starring Sutherland. From 1975 until 1986 Bonynge served as music director of the Australian Opera, the resident company at the Sydney Opera House. The conductor is also a leading scholar of 18th- and 19th-century vocal music— the bel canto works of Handel, Bellini, and Donizetti—whose revival in our time he and Sutherland did much to achieve.*

1952 *saw the first steps towards an Australian national opera when the New South Wales National Opera of Sydney and the National Theatre Opera of Melbourne agreed to pool their resources. Rivalries, however, forced the two ensembles to operate separately until the formation of the Elizabethan Trust in 1954, which led to the establishment of a new company, the Australian Opera. Now at home in the new Sydney Opera House, the company is continually renewing itself, especially through the nurturing of talented young singers and musicians. Contemporary Australian opera is also flourishing, thanks to the emergence of composers and interpreters of considerable merit. The originality of the Sydney Opera House lies in its ongoing program of musical performances for children and of fresh, untried works added to the standard repertory.*

FACTS ABOUT THE BUILDING
1973 *Jørn Utzon, Ove Arup, E.H. Farmer, Peter Hall, Lionel Todd, and David Littlemore, architects and engineers*
Capacity: 2,679
Stage: **length** 16.9m **height** 7.2m
depth 11.51m

Théâtre Royal de la Monnaie *Brussels*

THÉÂTRE ROYAL DE LA MONNAIE

Brussels - Belgium

1817-1819. *The theatre, designed by Louis Damesne, is built on the site of the Mint (la Monnaie).*

1855. *Fire destroys everything but the outside walls and the portico. The Belgian architect Joseph Poelaert reconstructs it in fourteen months, allowing the exterior to disclose nothing of the functions within, just as Damesne had decided. Poelaert has the pediment over the peristyle carved in relief by the sculptor Simonis and creates an auditorium with 1,200 seats. The new Théâtre Royal da la Monnaie is opened a year later with Halévy's* Jaguarita l'Indienne.

1985. *A radical renovation is called for and assigned to A.2R.C., Urbat, and to Charles Vandenhove. The overall height is raised by 4 metres and the roofline stressed with a broad band of cobalt blue. The entrance hall has a ceiling painted by Sam Francis and a floor designed by Sol LeWitt. The foyer retains its 19th-century red and gold décor, unlike the royal salon, where, within a white, contemporary environment, Daniel Buren graced the floor with his signature stripes and Giulio Paolini introduced Neoclassical sculptures. The red and gold auditorium remains the same, acoustically improved, and its capacity increased to 1,770.*

1986. *Inauguration of the renovated theatre on 12 November with Beethoven's Ninth Symphony.*

orn two centuries ago on the Quai aux Foins, Belgium's main opera house owes its name to the nearby presence of the old Mint, whose site would be taken over when a certain Sieur Bombarda rebuilt the theatre and reopened it in 1700 with a performance of Lully's *Atys*. In 1817, the architect Damesne began work on a second theatre behind the first one. It was in the new house on 25 August 1830 that a performance of Auber's *La Muette de Portici*, with its rousing call to arms, sparked a rebellion. Devoured by flames in 1855, save for the portico and the walls, La Monnaie was rebuilt a year later by Joseph Poelaert, who decorated the auditorium in a Louis XVI manner to please the taste of the ascendant bourgeoisie. This did not help the faulty foundations of the theatre, and the stage building collapsed not long afterwards. At the turn of the 20th century, La Monnaie gained an additional story, and then a new stage building in the 1950s, none of which satisfied a commission charged with determining the safety of the theatre. La Monnaie had to be either stabilized or closed. Launched in 1985, the renovation, like the one at Lyons a year later, scooped out the stage building so as to increase its height by several metres and add an attic,

whose wide band of blue enamel challenged the Neoclassicism of the whole. A structural frame of steel relieved the walls of the weight of the modernized stage machinery, as well as creating spaces for rehearsals and other backstage activities. Inside the theatre as well as on the exterior, the architectural collective known as

FACTS ABOUT THE BUILDING

1819 *Louis Damesne, architect*
1856 *Joseph Poelaert, architect*
1986 *A.2R.C., Urbat, and Charles Vandenhove, architects*
Capacity: 1,770
Horsehoe auditorium
1 orchestra stalls
1 ring of ground-floor boxes
1 balcony
4 tiers of boxes
Proscenium: **width** 12.6m, **height** 11m
Stage: **width** 21m, **height** 21m, **depth** 17.50m

"Entre Rêve et Réalité" sought a harmonious reconciliation of the past and the future. The auditorium, refreshed and acoustically improved, remains the red and gold affair designed by Poelaert, with its huge crystal chandelier, its ground-floor boxes, its generous balcony, and its two galleries. The public spaces and the royal salon, meanwhile, have been opened to the brushwork of Sam Francis and Sol LeWitt, as well as to Giulio Paolini's sculptures and Daniel Buren's zebra-striped marble columns, allowing the grand foyer to survive intact. Proof that intelligent modernization is sometimes preferable to building from scratch, the Théâtre Royal de la Monnaie still bears the stamp of Gérard Mortier, who, from 1981 to 1990, made Brussels one of the brightest spots in the operatic firmament. Stressing music drama and intensive rehearsal rather than stars, Mortier staged productions that were as exemplary as the theatre in which they appeared.

During the second half of the 19th century La Monnaie was known for its succession of major conductors, among them Joseph Dupont, Philippe Flon, and Silvain Dupuis. The house also staged the world premieres of several important operas, including Massenet's Hérodiade *(1881)*, Reyer's Sigurd *(1884) and* Salammbô *(1890)*, Chabrier's Gwendoline *(1886), and* Chausson's Le Roi Arthus *(1903)*.

1916-1918. *Richard Strauss conducts* Der Rosenkavalier *with a cast that includes the creators of the three female leads.*

Other world premieres: *Milhaud's* Les Malheurs d'Orphée *(1916),* Honegger's Antigone *(1927), and* Prokofiev's The Gambler *(1919)*.

1981. *Gérard Mortier succeeds Maurice Huisman and initiates an artistic policy of avoiding the "star system" in favor of well-conceived, intensely rehearsed productions.*

1991. *In April, Bernard Foccroulle takes charge, with Antonio Pappano as music director and Sylvain Cambreling as guest conductor. Under the new management, the star system continues to be resisted. The repertory is chosen without reference to the preferences of great singers on the international circuit. Of the seven new productions scheduled each season, one must be a new work by a contemporary composer (sometimes mounted in collaboration with another house): Pascal Dusapin in 1992, Philippe Boesmans in 1993, and Jonathan Harvey in 1994. The season also offers three revivals and one or two borrowed ones.*

Recent productions: *Strauss's* Salome *directed by Luc Bondy (imported from Salzburg), Verdi's* Falstaff *directed by Peter Stein, and Wagner's* Parsifal *mounted by Klaus Michael Grüber.*

Aalto-Theater
Essen

AALTO-THEATER
Essen - Germany

1959. *The Finnish architect Alvar Aalto wins the design competition launched by the city of Essen in Germany's Rhineland.*
1976. *Alvar Aalto dies.*
1983. *Construction begins.*
1988. *Inaugurated 2 October with Wagner's* Die Meistersinger von Nürnberg.

Alvar Aalto *(1898-1976). Trained at the Helsinki Polytechnic, from which he graduated in 1921, Aalto saw architecture as a means of reconciling nature and industry. In 1929 and 1933 he participated in the CIAM (Congrès International d'Architecture Moderne), where he formed close ties with the avant-garde (Le Corbusier, Moholy-Nagy, Brancusi, Braque, Calder), emerging as one of the forerunners of the democratic tendency whereby architecture, urbanism, standardization, and flexible habitat are all intimately linked.*

FACTS ABOUT THE BUILDING

1959 *Alvar Aalto, winner of Essen's design competition*
1988 *Alvar Aalto, architect of the built opera house*
Fan-shaped auditorium
Capacity: 1,125
1 amphitheatre orchestra stalls
3 balconies
Proscenium: **width** 17m, **height** 9.50m
Stage: **width** 25m, **height** 24m, **depth** 19.80m

M any are the theatres restored from the plans of long-departed architects, but the opera house in Essen counts among the few that were originally built after the architect's death. In 1959, Alvar Aalto, Finland's titan of modernist architecture, won the competition launched by the Rhenish city, at the heart of industrial Germany, with a fan-shaped auditorium derived from fundamental principles already tested in Helsinki. Working on a modest scale (capacity: 1,125), Aalto designed a low ceilinged auditorium equipped with overhead reflectors, to correct the acoustics, and giving the area of the orchestra stalls an asymmetrical plan. Not until 1983 did Essen finally decide to translate the project into architectural reality. Aalto having died seven years earlier, his widow watched over the building process, assuring the integrity of the master's revolutionary yet timeless ideas, while adapting them to the technology of the 1980s. The orchestra stalls defy all classical rules, being divided into two unequal parts, and the sinuous balconies, thanks to reinforced concrete, spring off the rear wall in successively bolder leaps. Deep indigo and mauve bathe the seats as well as the walls as they rise and engulf the ceiling in the same tonality. The architect reveals himself to be an intimist once beyond the entrance, the simplicity of which should not startle even those wary of modernism. Aalto, however, had a feeling for detail, for the subtleties of materials—combining wood, bronze, ceramic, marble —and even for the ergonomics of door handles. As for the stage, it conforms to a system developed west of the Rhine—that is, a main, revolving stage surrounded by two side stages and a backstage, all of which permits the movement of entire sets, designed and built in adjacent studios. Unfortunately, Essen's opera house remains Aalto's sole contribution to opera, a visionary exercise carried out with brio, though without suspecting that his theatre on paper would one day become a living theatre.

L'Opéra de la Bastille

**L'OPÉRA DE LA
BASTILLE**
Paris - France

1968. *Jean Vilar, Pierre Boulez, and Maurice Béjart publish their report recommending a new opera house for Paris.*

1982. *President François Mitterand authorizes the construction of "modern and popular" opera house and expresses preference for the Bastille as a symbolic site. A design competition is announced, eventually attracting 756 candidates.*

1983. *Carlos Ott is declared the winner on 17 November, by a jury convinced, it is said, that is was choosing Richard Meier.*

1984. *Work to clear the Bastille site is begun.*

1985. *The foundations are begun.*

1986. *The conservatives return to power, interrupting work for several months.*

1987-1988. *Stage equipment and interior architecture. Acoustical research, including sophisticated simulation techniques.*

1989. *Inaugurated 13 July, the orchestra stalls filled with heads of state for a gala entitled "The Night before the Day." Conductor: Georges Prêtre; director: Robert Wilson; cast: Teresa Berganza, Placido Domingo, Barbara Hendricks, Ruggiero Raimondi, Shirley Verrett. . . . The season would not open until September with* Les Troyens *by Hector Berlioz.*

The Opéra de la Bastille—almost like a re-run of the Palais Garnier—came into the world accompanied by a chorus of overheated debates, passionate crusades, and tricky politics. Curiously, the original initiative came from a composer who had never written a note for opera and who even had a rather low opinion of bel canto, Pierre Boulez. In 1968, however, Boulez, together with Jean Vilar and Maurice Béjart, signed a report declaring the urgent need to rethink the operatic scene in Paris. With Vilar, the notion of a popular theatre was never far from his mind, and it was with this purpose that, in 1982, François Mitterand announced a design competition for a new opera house. Though originally planned for La Villette, where the Cité de la Musique was to rise, Mitterand's "modern and popular" opera finally opened on 14 July 1989 on the Place de la Bastille, thus becoming a symbol of revolution in all its forms. Garnier in 1868 had prevailed over 171 competitors, but a century later the number of contestants for the big government prize was 756. Once again, however, it was an almost unknown architect, Carlos Ott, who won the jury's favor, even though rumor later had it that the jury had been mistaken about the identity of the winner. At the Bastille there was no problem about clearing the land, as there had been for Haussmann in the 19th century, since the new opera house was to occupy the site of a former train station, an odd, elongated lozenge of land, where the building would have on one side a railway viaduct, converted into a promenade, and on the other the circular Place de la Bastille. Here the swelling façade of the new building had to curve away to avoid a restaurant which had somehow managed to survive. In keeping with his time, Carlos Ott, like Garnier, chose to work in the official style. Surmounted by the opaque cube of the stage building and wrapped in gridded walls of glass, rather like Gropius's proposal for Erwin Piscator's theatre in Berlin, the Opéra de la Bastille stands sociably open to the world outside, whereas the foyers, with their broad overview of the city, have the slick, impersonal look of an airport lounge. All this changes, however, once the auditorium is reached, where 2,700 seats are spread over the orchestra stalls and three cantilevered balconies. The presence of pear wood gives a warm impression. Light is ingeniously suffused from three luminous wave-like panels

Born amidst intrigue, as much political as architectural, the Opéra de la Bastille had a difficult infancy, jerked first one way and then another by shifting changes of administration.

1989. *Daniel Barenboim is dismissed as music director. Pierre Boulez resigns from the planning committee. Herbert von Karajan announces that he will never conduct at the Bastille. Myung-Whun Chung succeeds Barenboim.*
1994. *On 14 October, at the end of a performance of* Simon Boccanegra, *Chung finds his turn has come to be sacked.*
1995. *In August, Hugues Gall assumes the directorship of the theatre. James Conlon becomes music director.*

A few statistics:

1990. *5 new productions, 3 guest [?] productions, and 90 performances.*
1991. *5 new productions, 5 guest productions, and 110 performances.*
1992. *7 new productions, 5 guest productions, 134 performances. Every new production is given 12 times. In addition to operatic performances, the theatre offers concerts, making a total of 220 events, which is close to the 1982 forecast calling for 250 performances a year.*

High points of recent seasons:

1990. *November, a new production of Verdi's* Otello *directed by Petrika Ionesco and a first performance in the house of* L'Histoire de Manon, *a ballet by Kenneth MacMillan.*
1991. *July, a new production of Mozart's* The Magic Flute *directed by Robert Wilson.*
1992. *February, first performance in the house of Shostakovich's* Lady Macbeth of Mtsensk *directed by André Engel. December, Messaien's* Saint François d'Assise *directed by Peter Sellars.*

FACTS ABOUT THE BUILDING

1989 *Carlos Ott, architect*
Amphitheatre auditorium
Capacity: 2,723
2 balconies
Multi-purpose hall: 600–1,000 seats
Animation theatre: 500 seats
Proscenium: **width** 19.50, **height** 12m
Stage: **width** 29m, **height** 38m, **depth** 23m

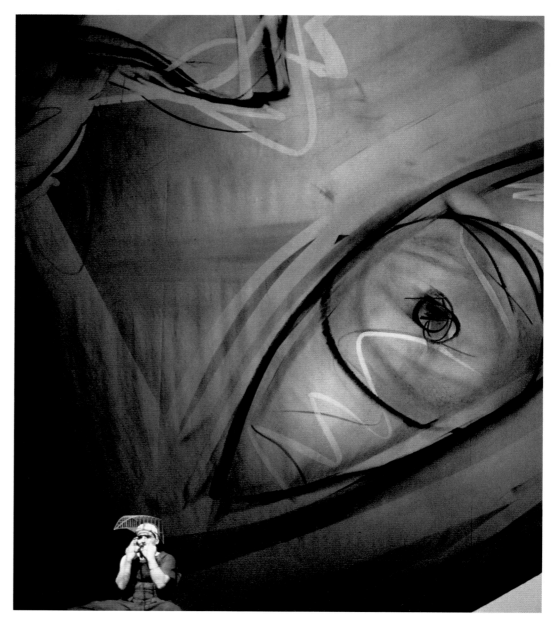

The Magic Flute, produced by Robert Wilson in July 1991 at the Opéra de la Bastille, Paris.

floated across the ceiling. The acoustics were calculated at length in a scale model. Behind the curtain painted by Cy Twombly, God's own plenty reigns. The volume of the huge stage has been replicated *nine* times so that designers, directors, singers, and dancers all work and rehearse at full scale. In this universe governed by state-of-the-art technology, entire sets roll on and off stage intact, all the way from the ateliers where they are assembled right up to the footlights. Overall a success, despite some human failures during the first few seasons, and built for the far more numerous tomorrows, the Opéra de la Bastille nonetheless bears scars from the power struggles surrounding its birth and infancy. One has only to consider the blind façade hiding the void left by the ex-future multi-purpose hall to understand how brutal the process sometimes was.

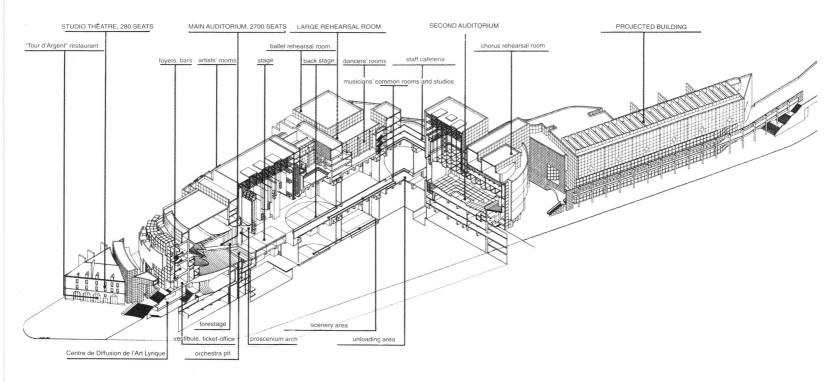

STUDIO THEATRE, 280 SEATS   MAIN AUDITORIUM, 2700 SEATS   LARGE REHEARSAL ROOM   SECOND AUDITORIUM   PROJECTED BUILDING

"Tour d'Argent" restaurant

ballet rehearsal room

foyers, bars   artists' rooms   stage   back stage   dancers' rooms   staff cafeteria   chorus rehearsal room

musicians' common rooms and studios

forestage   scenery area

vestibule, ticket-office   proscenium arch   unloading area

Centre de Diffusion de l'Art Lyrique   orchestra pit

Nouvel Opéra
Lyons

OPÉRA NOUVEL
Lyons - France

1756. *Jacques-Germain Soufflot's opera house opens 30 August. The elliptical auditorium within a freestanding building is one of the first in France.*
1831. *Antoine-Marie Chenavard and Jean-Marie Pollet erect Lyons's new opera house, which opens 1 July with Boieldieu's* La Dame blanche.
1985. *The city council votes 2 May in favor of rebuilding the opera house. Architect Jean Nouvel is appointed.*
1993. *Reconstruction ends 15 April, having retained the old façades and the arcades wrapped about three sides. The spirit of the restoration is consistent with the main façade and the grand foyer whose lights and gilding are reflected on a polished black-granite floor. The building is crowned by a steel and glass barrel vault that doubles its height. The arched ribs of the structural skeleton, all complete semicircles, are covered with a double skin, the underside of the vault being lined with curved glass faced in turn with silk-screened glass. The newly excavated basement contains a rehearsal hall as large as the stage itself. The adjustable orchestra pit can be covered to extend the stage, whose equipment is ultramodern and computerized. Overall, the usable space within the old opera house has been tripled. Inaugurated 14 May with Jean-Baptiste Lully's* Phaéton.

Once a theatre has been judged too small, the usual solution is to demolish it and make room for a larger one. In 1986, Lyons found another way, explored shortly before by La Monnaie in Brussels, which was to retain the original façades while enlarging everything within, a process that yielded the Opéra Nouvel, opened on 14 May 1993 and named for the architect, currently the most admired in France. For the second time in its history, the archiepiscopal see of ancient Gaul revolutionized the internal arrangement of its grand theatre. In 1756, Jacques-Germain Soufflot, the architect of the Panthéon, who had studied the Renaissance theatres of Italy and been consulted on several projects for French theatres, including the Comédie Française, built a theatrical gem on a site lying between the Rhône and the Saône, where he gave the so-called "French" auditorium its definitive bell-shaped, semicircular plan and improved visibility by the innovative technique of overhanging balconies. Condemned as too dilapidated in 1827, Soufflot's masterpiece was replaced four years later by a fairly uninspired building designed by Chenavard and Pollet, whose walls, in addition to Dardel's foyer, were all that Jean Nouvel would save a century and a half later. To create additional space, Nouvel excavated below the theatre and there introduced rehearsal studios as well as an another auditorium; more important, he doubled the building's height by crowning the old Neoclassical carcass with a huge glazed, steel-frame barrel vault, which, though worthy of the visionary Boullée, set off an explosion of local debate. Hidden away under this 20-metre-high structure are the stage flies and spaces for ballet, all protected from curious eyes and the greenhouse effect by thousands of silk-screened brise-soleils. Gleaming by daylight, the superstructure blushes softly by night, thanks to the magical lighting of Yann Kersalé, which glows more or less intensely according to the number of people inside, winking at the good burghers of Lyons. The interior, completely fitted out in glossy black, seems to float in space, the sense of levitation reinforced by a battery of escalators and safety stairs leading to "buffer zones" lined with red satin. Combining amphitheatre orchestra stalls with boxes tiered in the Italian manner, Jean Nouvel paid homage to the sumptuous past, even to the point of gilding the ceiling and drawing the

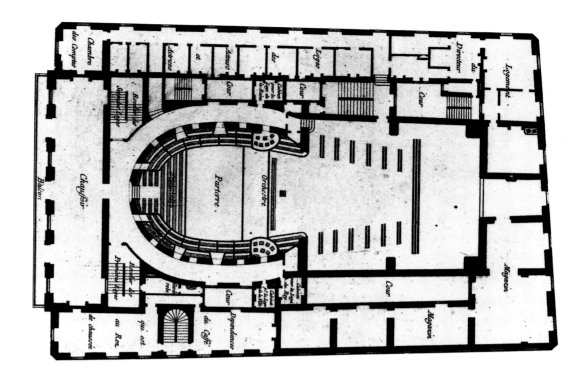

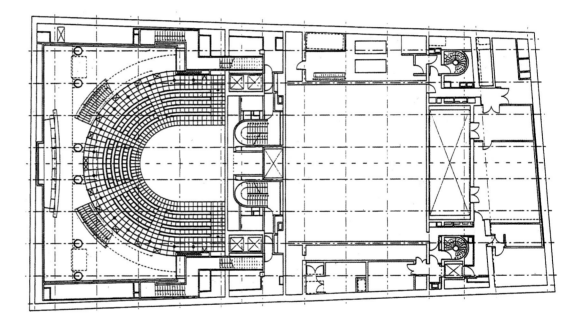

spectator into the décor through a network of optical fibers that pick out faces in the darkness. An architectural tour de force, in which the past has been successfully wedded to the future, Lyons's Opéra Nouvel is still trapped within its own spatial limits, since the expanded stage has come at the expense of both backstage and storage, so that sets arrive on to the stage directly from the street.

VII Opera Houses Transformed

Royal Opera House
Covent Garden, London

1857. *The Duke of Bedford, the owner of Covent Garden estate, recruits Frederick Gye, a rich merchant, to organize and manage the construction of the present opera house. Gye in turn engages the architect E. M. Barry, the engineers Charles and Thomas Lucas, and the iron-founder Henry Grissell. Flaxman's two statues and Rossi's friezes, salvaged from the old, burnt-down building, are re-used on the façade, left and right of the giant portico. Eight metal A-beams span the building from side to side and support the stage machinery. Three balconies and a tier of ground-floor boxes run completely round the U-shaped*

The first Covent Garden opened in 1732 close to the so-called "Piazza" of Covent Garden, on a site formerly occupied, as the name implies, by a convent garden belonging to the monks of Westminster Abbey. The inaugural work was Congreve's *The Way of the World*, and, apart from *The Beggars' Opera* and a few Handel operas, Covent Garden remained a venue dedicated primarily to plays for the next hundred years. The auditorium was completely reconstructed by Henry Holland in 1791–94. In 1809, following a fire, the second Covent Garden rose from the ashes of the first, to the design of Sir Robert Smirke. Now it became an opera house, whose manager, Charles Kemble, invited Carl Maria von Weber to compose *Oberon*, which had its premiere on the Covent Garden stage in April 1826. In the period that followed until 1858, when the present theatre opened, Covent Garden presented Maria Malibran in *La Sonnambula* and *Fidelio*, Adelaide Kemble in *Norma*, the company from Brussels's La Monnaie in *William Tell*, *Les Huguenots*, and *La Muette de Portici*, and an Italian troupe that gave London its first *Aida*, with Adelina Patti in the title role. On 15 May 1858, there was another disastrous fire, after which the third Covent Garden opened with Meyerbeer's *Les Huguenots*, and it was meant by the director, Frederick Gye, to be both a model enterprise and profitable. A model the theatre surely was for its architect, E. M. Barry, an apostle of the Industrial Revolution and metal-frame construction. Thanks to his advanced technology, Barry could suspend the ceiling, as well as the stage machinery, from iron beams and thus create a classic horseshoe auditorium free of all columns. As for profitable, Covent Garden would be much less so after Gye added Floral Hall next door, a little Crystal Palace that functioned

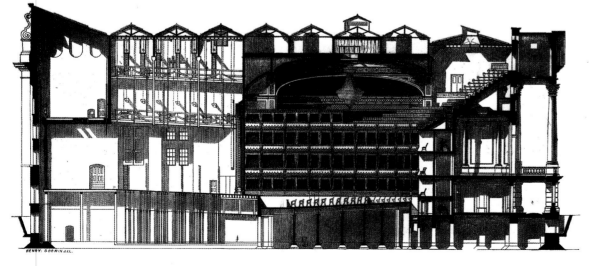

HENRY. GODWIN.DEL.

auditorium. A steep gallery descends to the third level. The double royal box and the box of the Duke of Bedford are at the side of the proscenium. The décor is by the Italian Raffaele Monti.

1858. *Inaugurated on 15 May with Meyerbeer's* Les Huguenots.

1899. *The architect Edwin O. Sachs builds an iron-and-glass enclosure on the portico terrace and secures the building with a fire wall and curtain.*

1951. *The porte-cochère under the colonnade is appropriated for the foyer.*

1982. *The backstage is both enlarged and extended.*

1997. *Future plans involve the demolition of buildings along Russell Street. A spacious foyer is to be installed in the renovated Floral Hall, the seating capacity of the auditorium increased, and the gallery integrated into the rest of the theatre. The public spaces will also be enlarged. The backstage will be modernized and a second auditorium created. A rough pastiche of one side of Inigo Jones's 17th-century Covent Garden Piazza is to be built. The campaign of building and renewal should be completed by the year 2000.*

Auditorium of the Italian Opera House, Haymarket, London, in 1809.

FACTS ABOUT THE BUILDING

1732 *Edward Shepherd, architect of the first Covent Garden Theatre*
1791 *Henry Holland, architect of the reconstructed auditorium*
1809 *Sir Robert Smirke, architect of the second theatre*
1858 *E. M. Barry, architect of the third theatre*
1899 *Edwin O. Sachs, architect of the iron-and-glass Crush Bar*
1982 *Jeremy Dixon and Edward Jones, architects of the backstage extension and renovation*
Horseshoe auditorium
Capacity: 2,174
4 tiers of boxes and balconies, 1 gallery
Proscenium: **width** 12.20m; **height** 14.80m
Stage: **width** 33m; **height** 36m; **depth** 24m

as a flower market by day and as a concert hall in the evening. Cursed with bad acoustics, it ended up a warehouse for sets and costumes. Inside the opera house as well on the exterior, Gye economized at every turn, particularly when it came to spaces reserved for the public. Barry, however, managed to endow the entrance façade with a Corinthian portico, to which the terrace with its iron-and-glass Crush Bar would be added in 1899. Despite two backstage renovations in the 20th century, Covent Garden, which had become the Royal Opera in 1892, could not approach the third millennium without working space sufficient to its ambitions. Extensive additions to the backstage area were made in the 1980s, but even more drastic alterations are planned for the late '90s. Jeremy Dixon was appointed architect in charge. A vast program of expansion is planned. Access will be altered, with the opera house and the new recital hall served by a huge double staircase in the form of an ellipse. At the same time, Gye's vision of opera combined with commerce will become a reality, through the many boutiques planned for the new structures to be built alongside the theatre. Tradition and modernity will cohabit in the same block, on the same scale as the surrounding area and without rupturing the unity of style so essential to operatic drama.

Joan Sutherland in Donizetti's *La Fille du Régiment*.

Covent Garden is the site of three successive theatres facing Bow Street.
1732. *The Theatre Royal, the first of the three houses, opens on 7 December with a revival of Congreve's* The Way of the World.
1735-1759. *Several operas by George Frederick Handel are premiered, among them:* Alcina *(1735),* Ariodante *(1735),* Atalanta *(1736), and* Berenice *(1737).*
1791. *Auditorium rebuilt by Henry Holland.*
1808. *Fire destroys the first Covent Garden Theatre.*
1809. *The second Covent Garden Theatre opens on 18 September.*
1826. *Carl Maria von Weber (1786-1826) composes* Oberon *for Covent Garden at the invitation of the theatre's director, Charles Kemble.*
1833-1847. *Covent Garden presents Maria Malibran and Wilhelmine Schröder-Devrient; Malibran sings in Bellini's* La Sonnambula *and in Beethoven's* Fidelio. *Also seen at Covent Garden is the company from Brussels's La Monnaie, which gives performances of Rossini's* William Tell, *Meyerbeer's* Les Huguenots, *and Auber's* La Muette de Portici.
1847. *Covent Garden becomes the Royal Italian Opera, beginning with a performance of Rossini's* Semiramide.
1858. *Fire destroys the second Covent Garden Theatre. The third theatre opens on 15 May with* Les Huguenots.
1892. *Now the Royal Opera House, Covent Garden presents Wagner's* Ring Cycle *for the first time in England, the performances led by Gustav Mahler.*
1914-1918. *Wartime closure.*
1939-1945. *Covent Garden does wartime service as a dance hall.*
1946. *Covent Garden reopens on 20 February. Rankl (1946-1951), Kubelik (1955-1958), Solti (1961-1971), Davis (1971-1986), and Haitink succeed one another as music director.*

Great moments at Covent Garden:
1952. *Maria Callas makes her debut at Covent Garden in* Norma. *Joan Sutherland makes her first appearance on the same stage as the First Lady in* The Magic Flute. *Kleiber conducts Berg's* Wozzeck.

1953. *Sutherland, still unknown, sings Clotilda alongside Callas in* Norma.

1957. *Kubelik conducts Janáček's* Jenufa *and Berlioz's* Les Troyens.

1958. *Carlo Maria Giulini conducts Verdi's* Don Carlos. *Callas sings Violetta in Verdi's* La Traviata.

1959. *Sutherland sings her first Lucia. The next year, after her debut at La Fenice in Handel's* Alcina, *the Venetians proclaim the statuesque Sutherland "La Stupenda," which she would remain for her huge international audience.*

1964. *Callas sings the title role in Puccini's* Tosca, *a role she would repeat in 1965 for the last operatic performance of her career.*

Principal world premieres:
Benjamin Britten's Billy Budd *(1951) and* Gloriana *(1953)*
William Walton's Troilus and Cressida *(1954)*
Michael Tippett's The Midsummer Marriage *(1955),* The Knot Garden *(1970), and* The Ice Break *(1977)*
Hans Werner Henze's We Come to the River *(1976)*
John Tavener's Thérèse *(1979)*

During its season, the Royal Opera, and the Royal Ballet which shares the theatre, give at least five performances a week.

El Gran Teatro del Liceu *Barcelona*

GRAN TEATRO DEL LICEU
Barcelona - Spain

1847. *The architects Miguel Garriga i Roca and Josep Oriol Mestres complete the opera house, built on an urban site surrounded by busy streets and flanked by blocks of flats. Inaugurated 4 April with an Italian cantata, a Spanish play, a group of Catalan dances, and several concert selections.*

1861. *The theatre burns down in April, all is destroyed but the vestibule, foyer, corridors, stairs, and the Liceu Circle. Josep Oriol Mestres takes charge of reconstruction.*

1862. *The rebuilt Liceu is opened 20 April.*

1994. *Fire breaks out 31 January, gutting the interior save once more for the Liceu Circle, a gem done up in the Art Deco style during one of the renovations, and a few old paintings and pieces of furniture. A vote has been cast authorizing the demolition of a dozen buildings so as to give more access to the theatre. Additional spaces are to be built on the sides, at the back, and under the stage, and hydraulic platforms installed, together with technical and administrative facilities. The reconstructed Liceu is scheduled to open in 1997 to mark the 150th anniversary of the theatre's foundation.*

O n 31 January 1994, Barcelona's El Gran Teatro del Liceu, for the second time in its history, went up in flames. The first opera house had been built with private funds in 1847 by the architect Miguel Garriga i Roca, who used a site provided by Queen Isabella, now wedged in between the busy *Ramblas* and large blocks of flats. The interior decoration imported from Paris would not long endure, because in 1861 fire swept through the house, sparing nothing but the vestibule and the foyers. For the reconstruction, money had to be raised through the sale of subscriptions to members of Catalonia's rising bourgeoisie, who thereupon became owners of the boxes they would occupy. Bourgeois too was the rather exotic façade, with its "mongrel" mix of Orientalism and Neoclassicism. Equally "neo," though Renaissance in derivation, were the salons with their parading allegories, the last of which were done only in the Franco era. The same revivalist style also prevailed in the gilt-edged auditorium, still huge even though its original capacity was later reduced from 3,500 to 3,000. Most of the habitués occupied places in the orchestra stalls, furnished with characteristic cast-iron frames upholstered in red velvet, while the privileged few took over the stage boxes, decorating them in their taste, so that neo-Louis XV met Gaudí in amusing juxtaposition. The theatre got its original chandelier back but remained smothered by adjacent buildings, which deprived it of decent side stages and of any access for

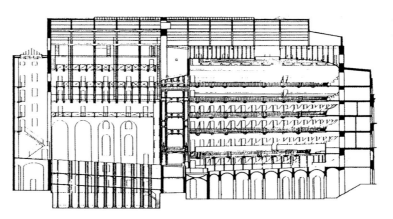

sets other than an ordinary back street. At the beginning of the 1980s Barcelonans launched a new campaign of restoration, firmly determined to liberate the building. Once again, however, fire proved faster than reform, but within a year and a

Victoria de Los Angeles

Born in 1923, this remarkable Catalan singer was only twelve when she entered the Liceu conservatory. She was just sixteen when she made her debut as Mimì in La Bohème. *On 1 January 1945 she sang the Countess in* The Marriage of Figaro *on the stage of the Liceu, launching one of the great careers of the postwar era. She created seven unforgettable operatic portraits: Manon at the Teatro Colón in Buenos Aires; Marguerite in* Faust, *directed by Peter Brook in 1953 at the Metropolitan in New York; Carmen at the New Jersey State Opera; Elisabeth in* Tannhäuser *at Bayreuth in 1961; Desdemona in Verdi's* Otello *at the San Francisco Opera in 1962. During a concert she gave in Frankfurt, de Los Angeles learned that Wieland, Richard Wagner's grandson, was in the audience. The next morning he offered her the roles of Elisabeth and Elsa at Bayreuth.*

The Liceu's pit has been graced by the finest conductors, among them Richard Strauss, Igor Stravinsky, and Felix Weingartner. Such world-famous Spanish singers as Montserrat Caballé, José Carreras, and Alfredo Kraus have made their operatic debuts on the stage of the Liceu.

FACTS ABOUT THE BUILDING

1847 *Miguel Carriga i Roca and Josep Oriol Mestres, architects*
1862 *Josep Oriol Mestres, architect*
1997 *Ignacio Sola Morales, architect*
Horseshoe auditorium
Capacity: 3,000 (less 10-15%)
5 tiers of boxes and balconies

half of the tragic conflagration of 1994 the architect Sola Morales presented plans for a Liceu, almost exactly reproducing the old one, except for the operatic scenes on the auditorium ceiling. Still, the flies are to be raised to 12 metres, offset in the auditorium by a loss of some 100 restricted-view seats. Conversation at smart dinners mostly turned on the number of private boxes, which was fixed at 71, only half the previous number. The privileged few will be even fewer in Catalonia's new temple of the arts.

New National Theatre *Tokyo*

1997. *Inauguration planned for October with a Japanese opera composed by Takeru and the Symphony Orchestra of Tokyo. Takeru has contributed enormously to the development of opera in Japan.*
Season 1997-1998: *Wagner's* Lohengrin *will be given in November, with the Tokyo Philharmonic in the pit. In January it will be Verdi's* Aida, *in a production designed by Franco Zeffirelli.*

In speaking of opera in Japan, one has a problem of definition. Long before the genre took shape in the Florentine academies, the classic Noh theatre had already experienced its Golden Age. But opera in the Empire of the Rising Sun was as remote from its European counterpart as a samurai is from an Offenbach gendarme. The spare, minimal stages on which the dance dramas of Noh or Kabuki play have little in common with the elaborate platforms essential to the luxury of a *Traviata* or the sorcery of *Robert le Diable*. It was only in 1903 that European opera—Gluck's *Orfée*, to be exact—first set foot on Japanese soil, and it would be another three decades before the natives began to develop a taste for bel canto. Despite the rapid development of local companies, regular tours by the great Western companies, and all manner of effort by Japanese institutions to help the public appreciate an alien art form, Japan would be one of the last Asian powers to erect a large, modern complex dedicated to opera. Finally, however, the New National Theatre will open in Tokyo in 1997, with a symbolic double bill composed of an original work by Takeru, updating an old Japanese saga, and a production of Wagner's *Lohengrin*. The first concern of the architect, Tokahiko Yanagisawa, was to insulate the building against the noise and vibra-

tions of a city caught in the stranglehold of its densely ramified traffic system. Silence having been achieved in the auditorium, Yanagisawa created an overall silhouette in which the volumes of the various parts are fully exposed, making its aesthetic consistent with the International Style already seen everywhere from Seoul to Helsinki. In other words, not a trace remains of anything specifically Japanese. Glass mosaic distinguishes the public spaces, squares of stone the backstage areas, round ones the shell of the auditorium, and sharp angles the stages, all adding up to another exterior without anything very dramatic about it. Inside, the two auditoriums also comply with popular norms: "Bayreuthian" orchestra stalls overhung by three balconies for the 1,800-seat hall dedicated to opera and ballet and a fan-shaped hemicycle with one balcony for the second hall, ready to turn its 1,000 seats towards modernity. As for the stages, they are designed in the "German" manner—that is, with lateral stages. Now, should *Madama Butterfly* succeed in reducing the Tokyo audience to tears, the graft may be considered to have taken.

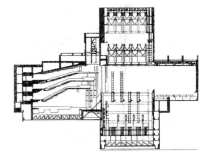

FACTS ABOUT THE BUILDING

1997 *Tokahiko Yanagisawa, architect*
Horseshoe auditorium
Capacity: 1,810
3 balconies
Proscenium: **width** 16.40m, **height** 12.50m
Stage: **width** 29m, **height** 30.50m, **depth** 24.50

Reference Section

Select Bibliography

IN ENGLISH

American Stage (The)
O.S. Coad and E. Mims, Yale Univ. Press, New Haven, 1929

Baroque Theatre
Margarete Baur-Heinhold, Thames and Hudson, London, 1967

Charles Garnier's Paris Opéra
Christopher Curtis Mead, MIT Press, Cambridge, Mass., 1991

Concise Oxford Dictionary of Opera
H. Rosenthal and J. Warrack, Oxford University Press, 1964

Contemporary Theater Architecture
N.A. Bowman and Silverman, The New York Public Library, 1965

Denkmar Adler, His Theatres and Auditoriums
C.E. Gregerson, Swallow Press, Athens, Ohio, 1989

Glyndebourne: Building a Vision
R. Runciman and M. Binney, Thames and Hudson, London, 1994

Great Opera Houses
P.C. Hughes, Weidenfeld and Nicholson, London, 1956

Great Theatres of London (The)
Ronald Bergan, Admiral Books, UK, 1987

History of the Royal Opera House, Covent Garden (A)
A. Saint, B.A. Young, M. Clarke, C. Crisp and H. Rosenthal, Royal Opera House, London, 1982

Louis Sullivan
H. Morrison, Norton and Co., New York, 1935

Modern Opera Houses and Theatres
3 vols, Edwin O. Sachs and Ernest A.E. Woodrow, Arno Press, 1896

Music, Acoustics and Architecture
Leo L. Beranek, Robert E. Krieger, 1979

Opera in America, a Cultural History
John Dizikes, Yale University Press, 1993

Other Taj Mahal (The)
J. Yeomans, Longmans, London, 1948 (on Sydney Opera House)

Theater Design
Georges C. Izenour, McGraw-Hill Book Company, 1977

Theatres, an Illustrated History
S. Tidworth, Pall Mall Press, 1973

Treatise on Theatres
Georges Saunders, Benjamin Blom, reprinted New York, 1968

IN FRENCH

Architecture et dramaturgie
Flammarion, Paris, 1950

Architecture et musique
Michael Forsyth, Pierre Mardaga (ed.), Liège, 1985

Deux siècles d'opéra français
Bibliothèque nationale, 1972

Grand Opéra en France: un art politique 1820-1870
Jane Fulcher, Belin, Paris, 1988

Grands travaux, grands architectes du passé
Jacques Levron, Editions du Moniteur, 1979

Graslin, Nantes et l'Opéra
Patrick Barbier, Coiffard libraire éditeur, Nantes, 1993

Histoire de l'Opéra
René Leibovitz, Buchet-Chastel, Paris, 1987

Histoire de l'Opéra en France
Francis Claudon, Jean Mongrédien, Carl de Nys and Karlheins Roschitz, Nathan, Paris, 1984

Histoire des salles de l'Opéra de Paris
Jean Gourret, Guy Tredaniel Editeur, 1985

Histoire des spectacles
edited by Guy Dumur, Yvon Bélaval, Paris, Gallimard, 1965

Opéra (L')
Edited by Pierre Brunel and Stéphane Wolff, Bordas, Paris, 1980

Opéra, 800 oeuvres de 1597 à nos jours (L')
Various authors, Ramsay, Paris, 1979

Opéra de Marseille, 1787–1987 (L')
André Segond and Eric Arrouas, Editions Jeanne Laffitte, 1987

Opéras d'Europe
Jacques Moatti, Florian Kleinefenn and Jean Vermeil, Editions Plume, Paris, 1989

Opéra et cinéma
Jean-Paul Bourre, Editions Artefact, 1987

Parallèle de plans des plus belles salles d'Italie et de France
Gabriel Dumont, 1764

Projets et divagations de Claude-Nicolas Ledoux, architecte du roi
Y. Christ, Editions du Minotaure, 1961

Rouge et or (Le)
Georges Banu, Flammarion, Paris, 1989

Temples de l'opéra (Les)
Thierry Beauvert and Michel Parouty, Découvertes Gallimard, Paris, 1990

Théâtre des origines à nos jours (Le)
L. Moussinac, 1957

Théâtre du Capitole 1552–1977 (Le)
    Auguste Rivière and Alain Jouffroy, Privately published, 1978
Théâtres, 4 siècles d'architecture et d'histoire
    Pierre Pougnaud, Editions du Moniteur, Paris, 1980
Trois siècles d'opéra à Lyon
    Bibliothèque municipale de Lyon, 1987

IN ITALIAN

Architetture per lo spettacolo
    R. Aloi, Hoepli, 1958
Duecento anni alla Scala 1778–1978
    Luigi Ferrari, Electa, 1978
Enciclopedia dello spettacolo
    Edited by Silvio d'Amico, Editions Le Maschere, 1954–56
Lo spazio, il luogo, l'ambito, scenografie del Teatro alla Scala 1947–1983
    Various authors, Silvana Editoriale, 1983
Museo teatrale alla Scala (Il)
    Giampiero Tintori, Electa, 1985
Nuovo teatro Regio di Torino (Il)
    Edited by Guido Bonicelli, Societa degli ingegneri e degli architetti in Torino, 1973

Storia e descrizione de' principali teatri antichi e moderni
    Giulio Ferrario, Arnaldo Forni Editore, 1830
Teatri d'Italia
    Giuliana Ricci, Bramante editrice, 1971
Teatri del primo novocento (I)
    Francisco Possenti, Lucarini, 1984
Teatro di San Carlo 1737–1987 (Il)
    Franco Mancini, Electa, Naples, 1987
Teatro La Fenice (Il)
    Manlio Brusatin and Giuseppe Pavanello, Albrizzi Editore, 1987

IN GERMAN

Opernhaüser
    Hermes Handlexikon, Econ Taschenbuch Verlag, 1983
Theaterbau-Aufgabe und Planung
    Gerhard Graubner, Verlag Georg D.W. Callwey, 1968

IN SPANISH

Teatros liricos del mundo
    Enzo Valenti Ferro, Emecé Editores, 1980

Addresses of Opera Houses

AMSTERDAM - NETHERLANDS
Musiektheather
De Nederlandse Opera
Waterlooplein 22,
1011 PG Amsterdam
Tel: (31) 20 551 89 11
Fax: (31) 20 551 83 11

BARCELONA - SPAIN
Liceu
Carrer Sant'Pau 1, baixos,
08001 Barcelona
Tel: (34) 3 485 99 00

BAYREUTH - GERMANY
Festspielhaus
Luitpold plat 29
Postfach 100 262
D. Bayreuth
Tel: (49) 921 787 80

BERLIN - GERMANY
Deutsche Staatsoper Berlin
Unter den Linden 7,
10117 Berlin
Tel: (49) 30 203 540
Fax: (49) 30 203 54 206

BESANÇON - FRANCE
Opéra-Théâtre de Besançon
(ancien Théâtre Ledoux)
Place du Théâtre
25000 Besançon
Tel: (33) 81 81 61 61
Fax: (33) 81 81 21 02

BOLOGNA - ITALY
Teatro comunale
Ente Automno
Largo Respighi, 1
40126 Bologna
Tel: (39) 51 52 99 01
Fax: (39) 51 52 99 34

BORDEAUX - FRANCE
Grand-Théâtre Municipal
Place de la Comédie
33000 Bordeaux
Tel: (33) 57 81 90 81
Fax: (33) 56 81 93 66

BRUSSELS - BELGIUM
Théâtre Royal de la Monnaie
Koninklijke Muntschouwburg
Rue Leopold 4,
1000 Brussels
Tel: (32) 2 217 2211
Fax: (32) 2 218 3527

BUENOS AIRES - ARGENTINA
Teatro Colon
Cerrito 618
C.P. 1010
BS AS Buenos Aires
Tel: (54) 1 382 2389
Fax: (54) 1 814 4369

BUDAPEST - HUNGARY
Magyar Allami Operahaz
Andrassy ut 22,
1061 Budapest
Tel: (36) 1 131 2550
Fax: (36) 1 131 9817

CAIRO - EGYPT
National Cultural Centre
Cairo Opera House
El Borg
B.P. 11567, Guézira
Cairo
Tel: (202) 34 20 601
Fax: (202) 34 20 599

CHICAGO - USA
Civic Opera House
20, North Wacker Drive
Chicago
Illinois 60606
Tel: (1) 312 332 2244
Fax: (1) 312 332 2633

DRESDEN - GERMANY
Sächsische Staatsoper
Theaterplatz 2,
01067 Dresden
Tel: (49) 351 49 110
Fax: (49) 351 484 2691

ESSEN - GERMANY
Aalto-Theater
Rodlandstrasse 10,
45128 Essen
Tel: (49) 201 81220
Fax: (49) 201 812 2105

GENEVA - SWITZERLAND
Grand-Théâtre
11, Bld du Théâtre
1211 Geneva 11
Tel: (41) 22 311 22 18
Fax: (41) 22 311 55 15

GLYNDEBOURNE - ENGLAND
Glyndebourne Opera House
Glyndebourne, Near Lewes
East Sussex BN8 5UU
Tel: (44) 1273 812 321
Fax: (44) 1273 812 783

HANOI - VIETNAM
Municipal Theatre
Rue Trâng tiên
Hanoi
Tel: (84) 4 25 43 12

HELSINKI - FINLAND
Suomen Kansallisooppera
Helsinginkatu 58
B.O. Box 176
00250 Helsinki
Tel: (358) 0 403 021
Fax: (358) 0 4030 2303

LISBON - PORTUGAL
Teatro National São Carlos
Rua Serpa Pinto, 9
1200 Lisbon
Tel: (351) 1 346 84 08
Fax: (351) 1 347 17 38

LONDON - ENGLAND
Covent Garden
Royal Opera House
London WC2E 9DD
Tel: (44) 171 340 4000
Fax: (44) 171 836 1762

LYONS - FRANCE
Opéra Nouvel
1, place de la Comédie
69001 Lyon
Tel: (33) 72 00 45 00
Fax: (33) 72 00 45 01

MANAUS - BRAZIL
Teatro Amazonas
Braça São Sabastiao SN
690 10 240 Manaus
Tel: (55) 92 622 24 20
Fax: (55) 92 622 18 80

MARSEILLES - FRANCE
Opéra Municipal
1, rue Molière
13001 Marseille
Tel: (33) 91 55 21 12
Fax: (33) 91 54 94 15

MEXICO - MEXICO
Palacio de Bellas Artes
Av Hidalgo 1, 3er piso, Centro
06050 Mexico
Tel: (52) 5 521 3668
Fax: (52) 5 521 6776

MILAN - ITALY
Teatro alla Scala
8, via Filodrammatici 2
I - 20121 Milan
Tel: (39) 2 887 91
Fax: (39) 2 887 93 88

MUNICH - GERMANY
Bayerische Staatsoper
Max-Joseph-Platz 2,
80359 Munich
Tel: (49) 89 21 85 01
Fax: (49) 89 21 85 11 33

MOSCOW - RUSSIA
Bolshoi
Pr Marxa 8/2
103009 Moscow
Tel: (095) 292 65 70
Fax: (095) 292 90 32

NANTES - FRANCE
Théâtre Graslin
1, rue Molière - B.P. 287
44009 Nantes cedex 01
Tel: (33) 40 41 90 60
Fax: (33) 40 41 90 77

NAPLES - ITALY
Teatro di San Carlo
Via San Carlo 98/F
80132 Naples
Tel: (39) 81 7972 111
Fax: (39) 81 7972 3069

NEW YORK - USA
Metropolitan Opera House
Lincoln Center
New York, NY 10014
Tel: (1) 212 362 6000

NEW ORLEANS - USA
Theater for the Performing Arts
801 North Rampart Street
New Orleans, Louisiana 70056
Tel: (1) 504 565 74 70
Fax: (1) 504 529 76 68

PARIS - FRANCE
Opéra National de Paris
Palais Garnier
8, rue Scribe
75009 Paris
Tel: (33) 1 40 01 17 89
Fax: (33) 1 40 01 94 01
Opéra de la Bastille
120, rue de Lyon
75012 Paris
Tel: (33) 1 40 01 17 89
Fax: (33) 1 40 01 16 16

PRAGUE - CZECH REPUBLIC
Národní Divadlo
Ostrovni 1,
11230 Prague 1
Tel: (42) 24 91 34 37
Fax: (42) 24 91 15 30

ST. PETERSBURG - RUSSIA
Marinsky Theatre
Teatralnaia pl.
190000 St. Petersburg
Tel: (812) 310 3202/310 4610

SAN FRANCISCO - USA
War Memorial Opera House
301 Van Ness Avenue
San Francisco CA 94117
Tel: (1) 415 861 4008
Fax: (1) 415 621 7508

SANTA FE - USA
Santa Fe Opera Theater
P.O. Box 2408
Santa Fe, New Mexico
87504-2408
Tel: (1) 505 986 5955
Fax: (1) 505 989 7012

SÃO PAULO - BRAZIL
Teatro Municipal
Braça Ramos de Azevedo
SN 010 37 010
São Paulo F.P.
Tel: (55) 11 223 30 22
Fax: (55) 11 223 50 21

SEOUL - KOREA
Art Center
1-5 Tongsung-Dong
Chongno-Gu
Tel: (822) 741 33 92

STOCKHOLM - SWEDEN
Drottningholm Slottsteater
Box 27050
10251 Stockholm
Tel: (46) 8 665 14 00
Fax: (46) 8 665 14 73
Kungliga Teatern
Box 16094
10322 Stockholm
Tel: (46) 8 879 14300
Fax: (46) 8 411 00242

SYDNEY - AUSTRALIA
Opera House
Bennelong Point
GPO Box 4274
Sydney NSW 2001
Tel: (61) 2 250 71 11
Fax: (61) 2 221 80 72

TOKYO - JAPAN
New National Theatre
1-1 Hon-machi
Shibuya-ku
Tokyo

VENICE - ITALY
La Fenice
Campo San Fantin 2519
I-30124 Venice
Tel: (39) 41 786 511
Fax: (39) 41 522 17 68

VERSAILLES - FRANCE
Opéra Royal
Château de Versailles
78000 Versailles
Tel: (33) 1 30 84 75 37
Fax: (33) 1 30 84 75 38
Théâtre de la Reine
Château de Versailles
78000 Versailles
Tel: (33) 1 30 84 76 41

VICENZA - ITALY
Teatro Olimpico
Piazza Matteotti
36100 Vicenza
Tel: (39) 444 32 37 81
Fax: (39) 444 54 66 19

VIENNA - AUSTRIA
Staatsoper
Opernring 2
A-1010 Vienna
Tel: (43) 222 51 444 0
Fax: (43) 222 51 444 2330

Sources of Photographs

Acknowledgments

Editions Plume are grateful to Sipa Press for their collaboration in the photography of Jacques Moatti and Florian Kleinefenn. They and their authors heartily thank the theatres, embassies and cultural institutes for the warm welcome they were given during the course of their research. The publishers would also like to thank the Bibliothèque Nationale, the Bibliothèque-Musée de l'Opéra National de Paris, the Bibliothèque de l'Arsenal, the Bibliothèque Forney, the Bibliothèque des Monuments historiques, the Bibliothèque du Patrimoine, the Musée d'Orsay, the Caisse nationale des Monuments historiques, the Réunion des théâtres lyriques municipaux de France, the foreign cultural centres in Paris, the French Institutes abroad, the Institut français d'architecture, the libraries and photographic services of the opera houses and municipalities, the Piano, A2RC, Jean Nouvel agencies and the Ecole nationale supérieure des Beaux-Arts de Paris.

Many thanks to the following people for their invaluable help:

Elie Bankhalter
Carina Blomquist
Bénédicte Bouges
Giacomo Bretzel
Jackie Camborde
Philippe Chiambaretta
F. Chiozzi
Elisabeth Connell
Constanza Corbeira
Leonard Da Selva
Thérèse Darras
Frédérique Delcroix
Elisa Delorme
Eaddy Derran
Peter Emmerich
Marie-Pierre Espugne-Darses
Latifa Fahmy
Gérard Fontaine
Jean-Paul Gousset
Italo Grassi
Barbara Grinberg
Siri Fisher Hansen
Catherine Heuls
Kristina Immonen

Jane Jackson
Martine Kahane
Marie-Claire Kerriou
Charlotte Kruk
Ada Kérouche
Isabelle Longuet
Jacques-François Marchandise
Susan Mathieson
Raquel Meade del Valle
Gérard Mannoni
Lucy V. Miller
Claudine Monteil
José Neistein
Corinne Quentin
Emmanuel Renoir
Nicolas Roger
Charles-Edouard Saint-Guilhem
Angelica Sanchez
Dean Shapiro
Elena Tarkahanova
Barbara Testoni
Christian Tourté
Regis Vasseur
Christian Wasselin

Index of architects

Index of singers, directors and musicians

First Published in Great Britain in 1996 by
Thames and Hudson Ltd, London

Copyright © Éditions Plume   1995

English Translation: Daniel Wheeler

British Library Cataloguing-in-Publication Data

A catalogue record for this book is available from the British Library

ISBN 0-500-01745-X

Printed and bound in Italy